A SEMINARY GOES TO WAR

ST MARY'S COLLEGE, OSCOTT
AND THE FIRST WORLD WAR

Judith Char

In honour he ... ...

In honour he died.

Faithful to God and Man.[1]

To Mike,
With good wishes
to a real military
historian, from
one merely
masquerading!
Judith

Oscott Publications

First published in 2015 by Oscott Publications

St Mary's College, Oscott
Chester Road
Sutton Coldfield
West Midlands
B73 5AA
Tel. 0121 321 5000
www.oscott.net

ISBN 978-0-9933991-0-7

Photographs: Front cover, Peter Harrington, back cover the War Graves Photographic Project, all other photos as individually credited.

Design and layout: Pixel Press

Printed by Genprint (Ireland) Ltd

Publishing Consultant and Index: Fergus Mulligan, www.publishing.ie

Contents

Foreword 5

The Dilemma of the War 6

Oscott's Military Tradition and the Impact of the War 8

The Arrival of Belgian Refugees 13

Mgr Henry Parkinson 15

Student Volunteers 17

First Oscotian Deaths 19

Priests Volunteer for Military Chaplaincy 22

Chaplaincy Appointments 23

Practical Difficulties 25

Fr Charles McDonnell 28

Mgr William Keatinge 29

Support from the Home Front 31

Fr Joseph Whitfield 34

'But what is one out here for?' 35

Bombardier John Molloy 40

Fr Herbert Collins 42

Fr George Craven 45

Sergeant Bartholomew Scanlon 47

Colour photo section 49

War Privations at Oscott 57

Conscription and the Issue of Exemption 58

The Drinkwater Brothers 62

Fr Francis H. Drinkwater 65

Lt Col Victor Mottet de la Fontaine 67

Oscott Reaches its Lowest Ebb 68

Final Oscotian Deaths 69

Lieutenant Joseph Arnold 71

Lance Corporal John Stokes 72

The Morale of the Chaplains 73

Catholic Social Teaching and 'after the war' 77

Demobilisation and Disillusion 78

Armistice Day 80

Post-War Reforms at Oscott 80

An Expanding Church 82

Mgr James Dey 84

The Catholic Land Association 90

Flee to the Fields? 93

Appendix 1
Oscotians commemorated on the Oscott College War Memorial 94

Appendix 2
Oscotian military chaplains 96

Appendix 3
Oscotians known to have served in the armed forces 99

Appendix 4
Oscotian family members among the war dead 102

Endnotes 105

Index 110

Foreword

This book began on Remembrance Sunday 2013, in the chapel of St Mary's College, Oscott, as I reflected on the thirteen men whose names are inscribed on the war memorial, and for whom we prayed. Who were they? Sons, brothers, friends and fellow Oscotians, of whom the present generation knew nothing. As the commemoration of World War One approached, it seemed fitting to try to recover some of their stories. From that began an exploration of the impact of the Great War on the lives of individual Oscotians, but also on the College itself, which was, inevitably, never the same again.

The primary source was the collection of letters sent to Mgr Henry Parkinson, as he strove to keep contact with the young men he had known as students and to keep the College functioning between 1914 and 1918. I am grateful to Fr John Sharp, Archivist of the Archdiocese of Birmingham, for access to this material and more besides. I am also grateful for assistance from the archivists of the Archdiocese of Westminster, the Archdiocese of Southwark, the Diocese of Brentwood, the Diocese of Salford, the Bishopric of the Forces, Downside Abbey and from the Curator of the Museum of Army Chaplaincy.

Invaluable online information has been gleaned from the British Newspaper Archive, the *Oxford Dictionary of National Biography*, the Commonwealth War Graves Commission and the Imperial War Museum. Photographic credits are due to Steve Rogers and his volunteer team at the War Graves Photographic Project and to Peter Harrington for the cover picture.

Personal encouragement and support, for which I am most grateful, has been received from Michael Snape, James Hagerty, from my colleagues on the staff at Oscott and the students who have lived with stories from the trenches at lunch for the last two years. Finally, I am happy to record my gratitude to Fergus and the production team at Fergus Mulligan Communications, for their efficient, effective and patient work in producing this, the first publication of the newly launched Oscott Publications.

Judith Champ
Oscott, October 2015

The Dilemma of the War

The declaration of war on 4 August 1914 presented English Catholics with complex dilemmas involving patriotism, morality and loyalty to the Church and the Pope. Public attitudes towards Catholicism in Britain were still not free of the Victorian prejudices that scarred earlier generations, and Catholics themselves were faced with difficult and often conflicting loyalties. Katherine Finlay summed it up succinctly:

> Given this situation, the Church needed not only to acknowledge the basic duties which Catholics owed to their country. More urgently, it needed to express the religious obligations which existed for Catholics and to demonstrate that these obligations did not contradict national loyalty but, rather, set patriotism within its appropriate framework, and, in so doing, purified it. Moreover, the Church needed to articulate its position so that it could adequately respond to non-Catholic suspicions of Catholic disloyalty. Indeed, loyal as Catholics understood themselves to be, this strongly-felt sense of Catholic patriotism was not always recognised outside the Catholic body. Instead, it was generally accepted that to be British was, more or less, to be English or at least 'Anglicised' and to be English was to be Protestant. Thus convincing the British nation of legitimate Catholic nationalism and expressing the compatibility of Catholic loyalty and national patriotism was no small task.[2]

Cardinal Francis Bourne, Archbishop of Westminster, took what his most recent biographer has called a 'considered and courageous' stand on the war, encouraging clergy to return swiftly from their holidays to attend to the needs of their people, directing the Catholic Women's League to respond appropriately, ('I am at my post; you should be at yours.') and opening Westminster Cathedral as makeshift accommodation for servicemen.[3] Three days after the declaration of war, Edward Ilsley, Archbishop of Birmingham, who had his residence at St Mary's College, Oscott, wrote to the clergy of the Archdiocese asking that, for the duration of the war, they use the Collect from the 'Missa tempore belli' every day at Mass.

The front and main entrance of Oscott College (Oscott College)

He was robust in his attitude to the war, describing it as 'a scourge in the hand of the Almighty for the chastisement of our sins'.[4] He expressed fears that, like the University of Birmingham buildings, Oscott might be requisitioned for use as a hospital. 'The authorities are commandeering right and left – houses, cars etc. They have taken the Birmingham University as a hospital with 500 beds – suppose we get an order one of these days to put up to 50 or 60 wounded here? I fear we shall have to send our students to their homes.'[5] Ilsley's anxieties were unfounded. Oscott remained open, and in many ways, life continued as normal. It would inevitably become a backwater during the conflict, but like the rest of the nation, the College could not fail to be touched by the loss of life abroad and privations at home, and by the moral choices to be made.

Oscott's Military Tradition and the Impact of the War

The Oscotian Magazine, published three times a year, continued to record all the normal College activities, with, initially, only a few clues as to the impact of the war; but as the years wore on and the death toll rose, these clues became more obvious. The internal life of the seminary was maintained as far as possible, including celebrations on 10 September 1914 to mark the twenty five years since the closure of the school at Oscott and the consolidation of priestly training at the College. This had been a major turning point in Oscott's history, with the final separation of seminary formation from lay education, a decision which many leading Catholic families deeply opposed.

*The sanctuary
of the chapel
(Oscott College)*

In the twenty five years since the closure of the school at Oscott, many lay Oscotians had gone on to careers in public service or in the armed forces. The military tradition of some of the families whose sons were educated at Oscott in the late Victorian period is clear from the list of alumni published in 1889 which records military honours among the old boys of the school. Several military heroes of earlier conflicts are commemorated on individual brass plaques in the Weedall Chantry at Oscott, including Lt Col George Bennett (Crimea), Everard Lisle Phillips VC (India), Lt Gen. Sir James Dormer (Egypt) and Maj. Gen. Victor Law (India). By 1914, a later generation of Oscotian schoolboys were either in the regular army themselves, or had sons who would be called into military service. *The Oscotian Magazine* during the war reported on the lives and deaths of these men with as much interest as those of the seminarians who volunteered.

Oscott subdeacons in 1907, left to right: Francis Sumner, **George Carlisle,** *Clement Krauth,* **Samuel Gosling, Herbert Collins, Joseph Lomax.** *Those in bold became military chaplains. (Birmingham Archdiocesan Archives)*

Theologians' football team, 25 October 1908. Francis Drinkwater standing at the end on the left and Charles McDonnell, seated in the centre in front of the priest, both became military chaplains. (Birmingham Archdiocesan Archives)

In December 1914, the first alumnus to be 'Mentioned in Despatches' during the 1914-18 conflict was noted in *The Oscotian Magazine*. Major General William Bernard Hickie KCB, was a schoolboy between 1876 and 1885, the son of James Hickie, also an Oscotian and a hero of the Crimean War. After leaving Oscott, he joined his father's regiment, the Royal Fusiliers and served in South Africa. He was in France for most of the 1914-18 war serving from Mons to Ypres and Cambrai, receiving the KCB for his distinguished service. Hickie came from ancient Irish stock, taking command of an Irish division from 1916 onwards, and was vocal in his defence of the Irish nationalist cause, roundly condemning the conduct of the Black and Tans in the War of Independence. Hickie was one of the last survivors of the lay school, living until 1950, and retained a great affection for Oscott, declaring himself more proud of captaining the winning Irish team in the traditional annual 'Great Game of Bandy', than of any of his wartime achievements.[6]

Nondescript Club, 10 November 1908, John Molloy stands at the end on the right, Charles McDonnell is seated on the end at the left, Francis Drinkwater is seated in the centre and Joseph Dwyer is seated on the ground. John Molloy served in the army and was killed, the other three served as chaplains. (Birmingham Archdiocesan Archives)

Few Oscotians suffered to the same extent as Edmund Maxwell-Stuart, who was a schoolboy at Oscott between 1870 and 1875; he and his wife endured the loss of four sons, Edmund, Henry, Joseph and Alfred, two of them in successive months in March and April 1916. Another son of an Oscotian who was an early casualty of the war was Lt George Archer-Shee, who served with the 3rd Battalion, South Staffordshire Regiment and died in action on 31 October 1914, aged only 19. George was not an Oscotian but his father, Martin, was at Oscott from April 1859 to June 1862, and 50 years on, despite age and infirmity, marked the anniversary of his leaving Oscott with an affectionate letter and determination to attend the College Feast on St Cecilia's Day in November 1912.[7]

George Archer-Shee and his father were the protagonists in one of the most famous legal cases of the twentieth century, immortalised in Terence Rattigan's play, *The Winslow Boy*, made into a classic 1948 film. Based on a father's fight to clear his son's name after the boy was expelled from Naval College for stealing a five-shilling postal order, it was inspired by the case of George Archer-Shee. As a cadet at Osborne Naval College in 1908, he was accused of stealing a postal order from a fellow cadet. His elder brother, Major Martin Archer-Shee, was convinced of his innocence and persuaded his father to engage lawyers. The most respected barrister of the day, Sir Edward Carson, was also convinced of his innocence and insisted on the case coming to court. On the fourth day of the trial, the Solicitor General, Sir Rufus Isaacs, accepted that Archer-Shee was innocent and ultimately the family received compensation.

Some believed that underlying anti-Catholic prejudice in the very 'establishment' institution of Osborne Naval College had played a part in the false accusation. George Archer-Shee has no known grave and is commemorated on the Menin Gate at Ypres (Memorial Tablet 35), on the war memorial in the village of Woodchester, Gloucestershire where his parents lived, and on the memorial plaque outside the Catholic Church of St Mary on the Quay in Bristol city centre, where he had served as an altar boy.

The determined emphasis in late Victorian Oscott and other Catholic colleges, on military heroism, the memorial plaques in the Weedall Chantry, along with the whiff of anti-Catholicism lurking around the case of George Archer-Shee, and the fact that fellow Catholics would be fighting and dying for Britain's enemies are all part of the complex context of Catholic patriotism and involvement in the war. These complexities were compounded by Pope Benedict XV's explicit and determined stance of neutrality and impassioned calls for a negotiated peace, and by the virtual civil war between Britain and Ireland, including the 1916 Easter Rising.

The Arrival of Belgian Refugees

The first visible sign of the war for most people in England was the arrival of Belgian refugees in the wake of the German invasion and occupation. This gave English Catholics the opportunity to be seen as patriots supporting the war effort, as well as loyal Catholics. Between August 1914 and May 1915, an estimated 250,000 Belgian refugees, mostly women, children and old men, and virtually all Catholic, fled to England, arriving in a pitiful and destitute condition. This fuelled the sense of righteousness in Britain's decision to go to war among Catholics and non-Catholics alike, and had a huge impact on some local communities, especially Catholic parishes.[8]

Belgian cities were flattened by enemy bombardment, among them Leuven (Louvain), where the buildings of the fifteenth century university and its world famous library were destroyed. Many English Catholic exiles during the Reformation had found shelter in Leuven and the connection had continued throughout the

Belgian refugee families fleeing from Belfort in the face of the German advance, August 1914 (Imperial War Museum Photograph collection Q53224)

generations. Its destruction profoundly moved English Catholic priests; many of those who volunteered for chaplaincy work had studied at Leuven or other continental universities.[9]

Fr William Barry was by 1914, the elderly, well-travelled and scholarly parish priest of Leamington Spa, who had earlier been on the staff at Oscott. He was faced with an influx of Belgian refugees, and recalled in his post-war memoirs: 'We had to provide almost immediately for more than a hundred Belgians, men, women and children, fleeing from famine and their ruined homes.'[10] A school was opened for the refugee children, and Barry recalled with some pride, sharing his 'modest' table with his counterpart from the cathedral at Mechlen (Malines), Canon Henri van den Broek. Barry was a well-known public speaker and preacher in the Midlands and after he had preached in 1915 at a Requiem Mass for the fallen in St Chad's Cathedral, a local newspaper commented that he had 'a special claim to speak to English people about this war, for he has been for many years a close student of French politics and life....He remembers vividly the last Franco-German war, and can tell interesting stories of life in many foreign countries of that time'.[11] Barry also published, in 1917, a substantial book in defence of the allied cause in the war, entitled *The World's Debate*. It is said that President Woodrow Wilson, who took the USA into the war in that year, ordered 1,000 copies.[12]

The relationship with Belgian refugees could be mutually supportive, and when in 1917, the parish priest of Kenilworth, Canon John Caswell, was too ill to continue, Canon van den Broek helped out in the parish. Barry preached at the funeral of his old friend, recalling how Canon Caswell had a reputation for keeping close personal contact with local men on active service, and 'acted indeed as a father to them'.[13] He was only one of hundreds of parish clergy whose lives and ministry were turned upside down by the war that came to their doors.

The parish priest of Lichfield, John Rowan, ordained from Oscott in 1900, had an army barracks in his parish, at Whittington. Just before war broke out he had begun building a church there, which was complete by December 1914 and proved a great blessing for the increased number of soldiers passing through the camp. On top of his normal pastoral duties the parish priest found himself with a much larger number of Catholic soldiers in his care, who were now preparing for war and possible death, not simply undergoing basic training. He also had an influx of Belgian refugees and four military hospitals in different parts of the parish. By the winter of 1915, he admitted that 'the strain is sometimes excessive'.[14]

Mgr Henry Parkinson

As Vice-Rector of Oscott from 1889 and then Rector from 1896, Mgr Henry Parkinson had known generations of Oscotian priests, as well as men who had not gone forward for ordination. He had always taken care to ensure that the seminarians under his guidance were conscious of the world they were called to serve, and worked closely with Fr Charles Plater SJ in encouraging priests to have a greater awareness of the social and economic conditions of the people among whom their ministry lay. He was a leading proponent of Catholic Social Teaching, based on Leo XIII's 1891 encyclical *Rerum Novarum*, and was the founding President of the Catholic Social Guild, and author of *A Primer of Social Science* (1913), which became the key text that set out the framework of Catholic Social Teaching.

Parkinson's task now was to maintain the ongoing life and mission of the seminary, whilst keeping students fully aware of the impact of the war on the country. In order that Oscott could be kept abreast of the international events, he insisted that the traditional religious readings during meals in the refectory were supplemented with accounts of the conduct of the war from *The Times* and the *Birmingham Daily Post*. Parkinson did not share the pacifist views of some members of the Catholic Social Guild and spoke at public recruitment meetings in Birmingham.[15]

Apart from Catholic Social Teaching, his other passionate concern was with the ongoing formation and support of priests and he was the founder and president of the Apostolic Union of Secular Clergy in England and Wales. He encouraged seminarians to join the Apostolic Union at Oscott, and kept in regular correspondence with members after ordination. Young priests in particular valued Parkinson's ongoing support: 'I know that you have very much at heart the welfare of those who are but recently set to do the work of missionary priests, and I rely on your prayers and those of my other friends to help me always'.[16] The writer, Fr Walter Amery was just embarking on priestly life in the Archdiocese of Westminster in 1905, and would later serve as a military chaplain for most of the war. Parkinson kept up, as far as possible, correspondence with men like Fr Amery and surviving wartime letters to him from serving chaplains reiterate their gratitude for Parkinson's continued interest and support, and reflect a deep affection for Oscott.

The Apostolic Union did not really take root in the other English seminaries, although Parkinson strongly advocated it at Oscott. One member, an alumnus of the English College, Rome, told Parkinson that he had only joined it, almost accidentally, because Mgr Charles Cronin, the Vice-Rector and an Oscotian, had mentioned it as he was leaving Rome.[17] The Apostolic Union kept Parkinson in contact with many of the priests who had been formed under his guidance. Branch meetings were, inevitably, more difficult: a meeting of the Birmingham Apostolic Union on 16 March 1916 drew only four members.[18] Nevertheless, a constant flow of reports from other diocesan branches, including Westminster, Hexham and Newcastle, Southwark, and from Scotland, came in to Parkinson at Oscott.

It was the correspondence between Parkinson and the Apostolic Union members that proved to be the invaluable link. One of the requirements of membership of the Apostolic Union was that each member would keep a monthly account of his fulfilment of the Ratio of prayers to which he was committed as an Apostolic Union member, and submit this to the president. The Ratio gave Parkinson a simple mechanism for keeping in regular contact with chaplains who were members. In October 1915, there were four Apostolic Union priests working as chaplains: Frs James Dey, Samuel Gosling, Charles Smith and Godric Kean, who was a priest of the diocese of Hexham and Newcastle, and the only non-Oscotian of the four. The Apostolic Union

Grave of 2nd Lt Joseph Bernaerts, killed outside Ghent in the last days of the war (Findagrave.com website)

secretary, Fr Augustine Emery, from his rural Staffordshire parish, commented somewhat naively to Parkinson at the time that, 'the war seems to have a wholesome effect on chaplains at least, judging from their letters'.[19] The reality was harsher. Fr Godric Kean, on one occasion in late 1916, sent a hastily scribbled postcard view of the river Somme, apologising for not sending his Ratio, as his knapsack had gone astray some three weeks earlier. He clearly had other things on his mind than reporting back on the regularity of his devotions.[20]

During the autumn of 1914, the number of students in residence at Oscott increased, as some men were unable to return to English Colleges in Europe, and seven Belgian seminarians were given a safe haven from their occupied homeland. The first of them, Joseph Bernaerts, a student for the Diocese of Mechlen, arrived at the end of November. Two brothers, Joseph-Marie and Victor Sempels returned as soon as possible to their own seminary in Belgium, while Robert van der Velde, Paul-Maria Goris, Honore Adolphe d'Hollander, Ferdinand von Trimpont and Joseph Bernaerts remained until 1915 or 1916. Some of their time was spent teaching Belgian refugee children billeted in Birmingham and nearby. Joseph Bernaerts, who left for active service in the Belgian army in January 1915, kept in contact with Parkinson through a regular correspondence in French, in which he repeatedly spoke of his fond recollections of Oscott as 'a house of peace' in the midst of war, and of his gratitude to Parkinson, not only for his Philosophy teaching, but for his guidance and advice about the life of a priest. 'I will never forget them, and they are with me in spirit'.[21] 2nd Lt Joseph Bernaerts was eventually killed in action by machine gun fire on the outskirts of Ghent in the last week of the war, on 5 November 1918, and is buried in Oudenaard Cemetery, Belgium. He is commemorated on the Oscott war memorial. R I P

Student Volunteers

Changes in the student body began to happen in the opposite direction, as the first students joined the hundreds of thousands who volunteered for Kitchener's army; those who had not received any of the clerical orders (subdeacon, deacon, priest) were free to join up. Seminarians were also recalled to their dioceses to help fill gaps left by clergy needed for other duties. Joseph Geraghty, from the Diocese of Menevia, suspended his studies to teach at St Mary's College Holywell, in place of its Rector, who took up work as chaplain to the North Wales Territorials. He was eventually ordained on 18 December 1915, and, in response to Parkinson's good wishes, thanked him for 'the benefits of all kinds that were mine during the four years life in the seminary', accepting his suggestion of joining the Apostolic Union.[22] John O'Riordan Browne was recalled by Bishop Casartelli of Salford to augment the depleted teaching staff at St Bede's College, Manchester. He was later ordained and in 1917 volunteered for service as an army chaplain. Fr Browne served, with a break to recover from dysentery contracted in the trenches, until 1919. His 'great gallantry and devotion to duty under heavy fire' earned him the Military Cross and Bar.[23]

William Farren, also a student for the Diocese of Menevia and former member of the Officer Training Corps at Stonyhurst, entered Oscott in September 1914, earning early respect and admiration for his 'genial disposition' and his devotion to the Mass and the Blessed Sacrament. He did not remain long and was one of the first Oscotians to go to the Front, volunteering for the 3rd Royal Welsh Fusiliers. By the spring of 1915 Lt Farren had been wounded in action and sent home. He returned to France but was sent home with a gastric problem. After further service in England, he volunteered again to go abroad, and eventually in September 1917 was admitted to hospital in St Omer, suffering from a nervous breakdown. For the last time he returned to Britain and on 17 March 1918 he died from double pneumonia in Seafield War Hospital, Leith, aged 25. Lt William Farren was the son of William and Isabel Farren, who lived in Caernarvon and he was buried at Old Ground 7, St Peblig Churchyard, Caernarvon. He is commemorated on the Oscott war memorial. R I P.

The grave of Lt William Farren in St Peblig Churchyard, Caernarvon (War Graves Photographic Project)

Mgr Parkinson's care for Oscotians, even those he had known only briefly, extended beyond the grave and he wrote to Lt Farren's mother requesting memorial prayer cards to distribute to his friends. She responded with thanks to him and to 'all who will remember dear William in their prayers'.[24] William Farren's story vividly illustrates the moral and spiritual conflict with which seminarians had to wrestle. At Ushaw, there was a clear policy that students should be involved in the war effort and by 1918, 93 seminarians had entered the forces.[25] Parkinson was much more concerned to keep seminarians where they were, if at all possible, but the young men continued to grapple with their consciences and their sense of duty over the issue of volunteering for military service. A letter to Parkinson from William Farren's home parish priest, Fr Frederick Furniss (himself an Oscotian), revealed something of those personal tensions, and also how, as Katherine Finlay expressed it, 'Catholic duty in some sense purified duty to country':[26]

> During the five years of my acquaintance with Mr Farren I came to know him intimately, to know him, in fact in some respects, better than he knew himself. For some considerable time before he realised his vocation to the sacred priesthood I had been very strongly impressed by the idea that his vocation was not for the world but for God....It may perhaps have seemed strange to you that, having realised his vocation, he should at the outbreak of war, have turned his back on it and joined the army. To Mr Farren, the war was not merely a war against Germany, but it was a war against the enemies of the Church. For, with a victorious Germany, he saw another code of 'May Laws' [the anti-Catholic legislation enacted by Bismarck in the 1870s] foisted not only on the Catholics of Germany, but on those of England, France and Italy. Hence he considered it his duty to go and fight for the liberty of the Church, since he was not finally bound to her by the vows of the subdiaconate. Of his gentleness, his charity and his kindly nature, I will not speak, for he has lived with you at Oscott.[27]

First Oscotian Deaths

The brutal reality of war began to impinge on life at Oscott, as in summer 1915 *The Oscotian Magazine* reported the first Oscotian death, that of Major Jasper Howley. Three generations of Howley sons had been educated at Oscott, eight in all from the same family. John and William Howley were at Old Oscott in 1803. John senior became a judge and was knighted and sent his son John to the school at New Oscott between 1840 and 1848. The second John's five sons (William, Gerard, Jasper, Richard and Henry) were all in the school between 1878 and 1889. Jasper was at Oscott from September 1881 to Christmas 1885, and was recalled as a quiet, inoffensive, neat, methodical and lovable boy. He was not a brilliant student, but plodding, industrious and persevering and took prizes in Classes III and IV. All five brothers were keen cricketers, and Jasper played for the First Eleven in 1885.

Three years after leaving Oscott, he followed his father's military footsteps by joining the Lincolnshire Regiment. He served with distinction in the South African War of 1900, where he was severely wounded. As a result of his heroism, he was twice Mentioned in Despatches and awarded the Distinguished Service Order. The DSO was instituted in 1886 by Queen Victoria for individual instances of meritorious or distinguished service in war. It was normally given for particular acts of heroism during active operations against the enemy, usually to those of the rank of Major or above. Major Jasper Howley was killed in action at the battle of Neuve Chappelle on 14

Maj. Jasper Howley, killed at Neuve Chapelle, was the first Oscotian to die in the war and is buried in Rue Petillon Military Cemetery, Fleurbaix. (War Graves Photographic Project)

March 1915. A fellow student, who went on to become a priest of Shrewsbury Diocese, Fr Joseph Chambers, remarked that he was 'a fine fellow and a good student'.[28] He lies in grave III.A.3 Rue Petillon Military Cemetery, Fleurbaix, Pas de Calais, France, and is commemorated on the Oscott war memorial. R I P.

Exactly a month later, on 14 April, a schoolmate of Jasper Howley, Lt Col Thomas Xavier Britten became the second Oscotian, and the highest ranking military officer from the school, to die. He was at Oscott between 1882 and 1886 and followed a similar path in life to that of his schoolfriend. He also came from a military family, being the son of the late Maj. General Britten of the Indian Army, and was born in India. He seems to have had a similar temperament to his friend Howley, but achieved more distinction in his studies, taking the 1st prize in class II, a Silver Examination medal and special prize for history in 1885. In 1886 he took the class prize in Rhetoric and the Oscotian Society prize for Maths, and passed the preliminary army exams for entry to Sandhurst. Britten began his career as a Lieutenant in the Gloucestershire Regiment, but died as Lt Colonel in the 110th Mahratta Light Infantry. He received wounds at Shaiba in the Persian Gulf, from which he died on 14 April 1915, aged 48. The same Fr Chambers recalled that 'Thomas Britten was a fine character, esteemed by professors and fellow students. His name deserves remembrance.'[29] Lt Col Thomas Xavier Britten lies in grave III.G.1, Basra War Cemetery, in present day Iraq and is commemorated on the Oscott war memorial. R I P. The Basra Commonwealth War Graves Cemetery lies in ruins, as a result of the ongoing modern conflicts in Iraq.

From 1915 onwards *The Oscotian Magazine* was reporting further seminary volunteers going into the armed forces, including James McKenna, Christopher Gilshennan and Leslie Gardner who went on to serve as a Lieutenant in the Royal Army Medical Corps. Among others who went directly from Oscott to the war were James Bligh, who joined the Royal Fleet Auxiliary, Jerome Coleman and James Lewis who both joined the Royal Garrison Artillery, Leonard Ross who became a Sub-Lieutenant in the Royal Naval Volunteer Reserve and Michael Russell who served in the Royal Naval Division, all of whom left in 1917, and William Mann who left in 1918 to join the Royal Marine Artillery.

Thousands of Catholics volunteered for the armed services, particularly, though not exclusively, in the Irish, Lancashire and North East regiments. English and Irish Catholics responded readily to the call to arms to defend Catholic Belgium against the aggressor and to demonstrate Catholic loyalty to the British Empire at a time when Catholics, and particularly Irishmen, were regarded with suspicion if not outright hostility.[30] Chaplains of all denominations were quickly in demand. At the start of the war there were only 117 military chaplains of any denomination, including seventeen Catholic priests. There was an immediate rush of priests volunteering to join Kitchener's troops, but only seven priests accompanied the British Expeditionary Force in 1914.[31] Clearly this was woefully inadequate but by late September the number had only risen to twelve. Within two weeks of the declaration of war, over 100 priests had applied to serve as military chaplains.[32]

Priests Volunteer for Military Chaplaincy

During the first winter of the war a growing number of priests accompanied troops into action, reflecting not only a change of heart by the government but the fact that the number of Irish troops meant that Catholics were disproportionately represented in the British Army. The matter was raised in the press and Parliament, and with some reluctance, the government sanctioned a large increase in the permitted number of Catholic chaplains. In November 1914 the government authorised a Catholic chaplain for every Irish regiment or battalion that was predominantly Catholic and for the rest of the war it proved difficult for the Church to meet its quota of priests. As late as September and October 1918, there was a shortfall of ninety chaplains, and bishops were receiving desperate pleas from the Senior Chaplain's Office to release priests for service.[33] Special pleading was often used on behalf of men like Fr Randolph Traill, an Oscotian priest of Birmingham Archdiocese who volunteered at the age of 53 and went on to serve in France for a year and a half. 'I have not met him personally, but I know a great deal about him and I am sure he would be a most suitable man, although probably only for base duty. With our present shortage, I should be most grateful if you make this a special case, in spite of his years, but, of course, do not want to make it a precedent'.[34]

Volunteering for chaplaincy service brought Catholic priests into an unprecedentedly close relationship with civil authority, with a potential clash between the role of the Church and military regulation. This could have tragic consequences: the first chaplain to die in the war was Fr William Flinn who persuaded a reluctant commanding officer to allow him to disembark with the men onto the beaches of Gallipoli in 1915 and was killed almost instantly. This was an instance of the desire of priests to endure whatever the men in their care faced, and the fighting men often took great pride in the fact that 'their padre' was with them in the thick of battle.[35] Whether this was the most effective place for chaplains was hotly debated throughout the war.

It was largely decided by the priests themselves according to local circumstances. Bishop William Keatinge, who had authority over Catholic military chaplains, maintained that chaplains should say Mass and hear confessions at every possible opportunity, but judgements had to be made on the ground as to the best place for this, and the letters of chaplains reveal the variety of locations in which sacraments were celebrated. Proximity to the front and to the heat of battle was not necessarily desirable. Apart from the physical dangers, which could remove a chaplain instantly, or leave him vulnerable to capture, it was rarely possible to administer the sacraments to the dying in the midst of the fighting and a chaplain could be pinned down to a single location, limiting his availability to men in need. The primary task, wherever possible, was to prepare the men sacramentally and spiritually before the battle, for what lay ahead in the coming hours or days. Reaching the largest number of men in danger of death was paramount, and for this reason, general absolution was frequently given before a battle.

Chaplaincy Appointments

Priests were commissioned as temporary chaplains for one year, which could be extended or terminated by agreement. A high proportion of the Catholic chaplains were from religious orders, mainly the Benedictines and Jesuits (40%), a further 40% came from English and Welsh dioceses and the remaining 20% from Scottish and Irish dioceses. The vast majority served with the army. Only forty Catholic naval chaplains were appointed during the course of the war because of the practical difficulties of committing a priest to a long tour of duty where the crew were predominantly Protestant, except on all but the largest ships.[36] One experienced naval chaplain with pre-war service, Fr Edward Mostyn, found himself serving as a wartime chaplain, not on board ship but in France, Italy and Turkey.[37] Probably because of the lack of spiritual care available, Catholics appear to have been actively discouraged from joining the Royal Navy.[38]

Among the few naval chaplains was Fr Joseph Dwyer, an Oscotian priest of Birmingham Archdiocese, ordained in 1913. He served on board *HMHS*

Landovery Castle in the Mediterranean in 1916 but wanted greater activity. He hoped for a posting to France but was sent to Macedonia where he contracted malaria that eventually killed him, aged 36, in 1923. He was much loved as a chaplain and would try to alleviate the monotony of the soldiers' lives and perhaps his own, by organising cricket, tennis, football and even golf for them, near Salonika whilst reminding them of the burdens endured in that same land by St Paul.[39] After demobilisation in 1919 he was appointed for a time to teach at Cotton College and then in parishes in Leamington and Dudley. Remembered by his contemporaries as a 'brilliant' student, but also as a man of great holiness, his advice to fellow priests was always: 'Keep your soul; think and do the thing that is right, and as long as you do this, be afraid of nothing.'[40] He died with a reputation as a priest with 'an unfailingly kindly spirit to all with whom he came into contact, and a readiness to help, no matter what their difficulty may be'.[41]

Another victim of the often random nature of chaplaincy postings was Fr Eric Green, an Oscotian from the Archdiocese of Westminster. Despite insisting that, 'I am afraid I should be little use as a naval chaplain'[42] he was posted to the Royal Naval Division, formed in September 1914. It consisted of men brought together from the Royal Naval Reserve, Royal Fleet Reserve, Royal Naval Volunteer Reserve, a brigade of Royal Marines, Royal Navy and Army personnel and fought on land alongside the Army. Green was in France and Gallipoli, was injured in late 1915 and resigned his commission in March 1917.

Most of the chaplains extended their service beyond the first year and some met the same fate as the men to whom they ministered. During the course of the war some 810 Catholic chaplains served and on Armistice Day in 1918, 649 were recorded as being deployed, alongside 1,985 Church of England, 302 Presbyterian and some 520 Free Church men.[43] The official figures record that 166 army chaplains died during the war, comprised of ninety eight Church of England, eleven Presbyterian, thirty four Roman Catholic and twenty three Free Church men.[44] According to a post war account by Cardinal Francis Bourne, the number of Catholic chaplains was disproportionate to the number of serving Catholics during the war. Bourne suggested that Catholics serving in the forces were never more than 15% of the total, whilst the number of Catholic chaplains exceeded 25% of the total. The figures were probably more like 6-11% of Catholics under arms and Catholic chaplains forming around 19% of the total; Bourne was broadly correct in his assertion, but, of course, the Catholic chaplains were stretched across the battlefields, seeking out the more scattered distribution of Catholic soldiers.

Practical Difficulties

All chaplaincy applications were handled through the Archdiocese of Westminster, accompanied by a recommendation from the priest's own bishop, but complications often arose in relation to appointments. At the start of the war, Fr Charles Smith was refused permission by the Bishop of Plymouth, despite requests by his brother and a local Catholic Colonel, partly because proper procedures had been ignored, and because of the bishop's own difficulty in keeping parishes manned. Smith had spent six months at Oscott in 1909 and was ordained for the Archdiocese of Birmingham, but after two years was taken on by Plymouth, as he had family connections in the south-west. Bishop Kiely did not want to lose 'a very accomplished priest and a zealous worker', but when Smith applied for release a second time in January 1915, the bishop told Bourne that he did 'not like to say no'. Smith declared himself 'in seventh heaven' and eagerly told Mgr Manuel Bidwell, who handled applications through Archbishop's House, Westminster, that he spoke some French, was used to riding on horseback and had some medical knowledge, 'so I feel that I should be useful at the front, where I wish to go as soon after the 28th as possible'. On 28 January, he had organised a concert to raise funds for Belgian refugees, so wished to see it to completion.[45]

The practical arrangements for chaplaincy appointments through the War Office were not always clearly understood. Complications ensued when Smith's parish priest wrote directly to Cardinal Bourne, requesting Smith's appointment to a particular division, supposedly about to leave for the Front. The local Catholic Colonel intervened again, trying to 'pull strings' to get Smith appointed to a division that he knew to be commanded by a Catholic, to whom he proposed to write on Smith's behalf. It did not stop there; in July 1915, a Major Fuller, of the General Staff at the War Office and an old boy of the same public school as Smith, wrote asking Mgr Bidwell if Smith could be appointed swiftly. 'As he is young and active and knows many of the Beaumont boys, I should consider it a great kindness if you could put forward his name when the next vacancy occurs'. Smith had clearly become frustrated by inaction, after having been in the army for two months but not sent to the Front, while appeals for chaplains were still being published in the press and he pestered Bidwell himself in June 1915. A note on this letter indicates that he had, in fact, just been appointed.[46]

Chaplain conducting a burial service on the battlefield near Ovillers, mid-July 1916 (Imperial War Museum Photograph Collection IWM Q 820)

Posted with the 21st and 23rd Field Ambulance, Smith certainly made his presence felt during 1916, insisting on providing Mass for hundreds of Bavarian Catholics in prisoner of war camps and arguing vigorously with the Church of England chaplain over the question of burials. It seems that an overly officious Anglican padre was insisting that all the war dead should be buried together by him. Smith was furious. 'I am perfectly sick of the way in which the Church of England deem it fit to appropriate every "body" they can snatch and bury it, regardless of the religion of the poor dead man. Is it not possible for a general order to be issued preventing them from taking all charge of the corpses of people killed, to the exclusion of everyone else?'[47]

There are many examples of the tension between Catholic chaplains and the Church of England that Charles Smith encountered, revealed in comments such as those of Fr Joseph Whitfield about a fellow chaplain: 'I may add without hesitation that no Church of England chaplain did any work which, either for strenuousness, length of time or dangerousness can be compared with that of Fr Colley'.[48] The desirability of Charles Smith, as Assistant Principal Chaplain, being appointed a

Domestic Prelate, giving him the title of Monsignor, is telling. It would give him 'a position in the eyes of military authorities and others which would help to counteract the Church of England titles – archdeacons, canons etc – one of which his Church of England counterpart in the army has, and it would be of much value from the point of view of keeping the Catholic flag flying'.[49] There is no doubt that the Catholic chaplaincy felt the need to assert its distinctive position and equality of status with the Church of England men and to ensure that the army recognised the particular mission of the Catholic priest and the authority of the Church in wartime.

Charles Smith was Mentioned in Despatches five times and in June 1917 was awarded the DSO, with a commendation that read: 'His devotion to duty and self-sacrifice have been a splendid example to all ranks during the past twenty two months. He was indefatigable in his work for the wounded under heavy shell fire'.[50] Smith was appointed Assistant Principal Chaplain in 1917 and in 1919 awarded the CBE, and continued to serve as a chaplain across the world. Until Henry Parkinson's death in June 1924, Smith and he kept up a monthly correspondence as he assiduously submitted his monthly Ratio as a member of the Apostolic Union.

It is clear from Smith's short but informative letters from postings in Baghdad, Egypt and China and lengthy journeys in between, that Parkinson's letters were a lifeline, keeping him in contact with the normality of life in England, with events great and small at Oscott, including the state of the College orchestra, a drowning in the bathing pond and the arrival of electric lighting in 1923. They shared a love of music, and Smith told Parkinson 'as a great secret' that he had privately donated the organ to the newly built Buckfast Abbey in his native Devon, in memory of his sister.[51]

Charles Smith retired from the army as Principal Chaplain in 1930. He then offered his services to the Diocese of Northampton and his army gratuity and pension enabled the completion of the new church in Beaconsfield, the parish church of G.K. Chesterton.[52] Smith extended the church, with fine Nuttyens stained glass, as a memorial to Chesterton. He died, aged 81 in December 1954, and was buried at his beloved Buckfastleigh in Devon.[53]

Fr Charles McDonnell

Fr Charles McDonnell, a priest of the Archdiocese of Birmingham, ordained in 1911, was teaching at Cotton College before the war. Along with his friend Fr Francis Lockett he volunteered for service as chaplain for the eight weeks of their summer school holiday in 1915. This was not taken up, but early in the following year McDonnell was assured by Archbishop Ilsley that be believed him to be 'fully qualified to undertake that duty' and gave him permission to volunteer as a chaplain 'for the duration'. Although the need for chaplains was urgent and Ilsley gave McDonnell leave to depart from Cotton almost immediately, on 15 January the correspondence between McDonnell, his Archbishop and Westminster reveals the difficulties of communication that delayed appointments. By the middle of February, although Ilsley and Bourne both supported McDonnell's application, he had heard nothing from the War Office and was advised not to do anything about getting his kit until matters were officially confirmed. Finally, in the middle of March, he was able to inform Mgr Bidwell that he had been appointed as chaplain in the Mediterranean and was about to leave for Egypt. Later in the year he applied successfully for a transfer to France. His elderly mother was losing her home and he was the only family member in a position to find and maintain a home for her. He was transferred to France at the end of September 1916.[54]

From early 1917 McDonnell was temporarily posted to chaplaincy service with the 10th Battalion, Royal Dublin Fusiliers, so was ministering to a largely Catholic battalion, where the men turned up for the Rosary every evening and for daily Mass as often as they could. Like so many chaplains he had to make the best use of wrecked village churches all over the battlefields. One church in his village had been used as a billet for the men, but he was able to celebrate Mass in the other, 'although there is not a window left in it'. The conditions in which he found himself were extreme: 'On two mornings it was so cold that when I consumed the Precious Blood I found that ice had formed in the chalice. Of course, the village is under shellfire, and one often says Mass to the accompaniment of our guns and Bosche shells. The thaw has come and now we have begun to wallow in mud again'.[55] McDonnell was regarded in his home diocese as a young man of great promise, but he died suddenly as parish priest of St Patrick's Wolverhampton, aged only 44, in March 1927. His obituary described him as a man of 'ready friendliness and large-hearted disposition, which broke down any obstacles of shyness or reserve in others'.[56]

Mgr William Keatinge

Cardinal Bourne was directly responsible to the military authorities for appointments but he insisted that his authority over the chaplains superseded that of the War Office.[57] Clashes inevitably happened between civil and ecclesiastical authority but also between dioceses and the chaplaincy office and particularly between Irish and English Episcopal jurisdiction. The senior Catholic Chaplain who went with the British Expeditionary Force was Mgr William Keatinge. In the urgent restructuring of chaplaincy provision in November 1914, an Irish Presbyterian was appointed Principal Chaplain to the Forces, with Keatinge as Assistant Principal Chaplain and Senior Roman Catholic Chaplain. Each denomination remained independent in organisation and deployment.

Keatinge appointed a Downside monk, Dom Stephen Rawlinson, as Principal Assistant Chaplain for the Western Front. His papers reveal much of the day to day administration of the chaplains and their work. Rawlinson had volunteered in August 1914 and gone to France at once and his distinguished record plus Keatinge's prior knowledge of him, meant that within a year he was appointed Keatinge's assistant and right-hand man. Keatinge and Rawlinson brought a high degree of skill and organisation to what had been fairly chaotic, by 'issuing guidelines and instructions to chaplains, keeping a close watch on those who were unable to maintain the high standards they demanded, and resolving the many difficulties thrown up by the circumstances of war, personal idiosyncracies, misunderstandings and failures of those with whom they were called to work'.[58]

Typical of the issues with which Rawlinson had to deal was the tetchy correspondence between Fr Young in the Senior Chaplain's Office and one of the Oscotian chaplains, Fr Samuel Gosling, serving with the 3rd South Midland Ambulance Service in the spring of 1916. Gosling had been requested, in the normal way, to sign on for a further year of service but was reluctant to do so unless he was guaranteed a period of leave to deal with 'certain private family affairs'. All leave was, at the time, embargoed and Gosling clearly felt aggrieved, claiming that other chaplains had been given leave on the expiry of their first year's service. The Senior Chaplain's Office needed an immediate answer as to his signing on for a further year and could not guarantee leave nor, if he resigned in order to deal with his family business and reapplied, that he would be accepted. In fact, leave was not granted by the Senior Chaplain's Office, but by the local

From October 1917 Bishop William Keatinge served with distinction as bishop in charge of appointing and deploying chaplains. (Bishopric of Forces Archives)

military commander at divisional level and as Gosling's final letter indicated, sent from his home in Newcastle under Lyme, he got what he wanted.[59]

Keatinge was eventually appointed as a military bishop or *episcopus castrensis*, with effective authority over chaplaincy appointment and organisation from October 1917.[60] Many years later, when Keatinge finally retired in 1935, Cardinal Eugenio Pacelli, later Pope Pius XII, told Cardinal Hinsley, Bourne's successor at Westminster, that the British Legate had assured the Holy See that the British Government 'would be very pleased to see the arrangement inaugurated in 1917, and which has worked so satisfactorily, continue'. As far as His Majesty's Government was concerned, Keatinge's appointment had been 'an unqualified success'. Rome was equally satisfied with what Keatinge had achieved. The only issue the Holy See wanted Hinsley to resolve with the government was that payment for Keatinge's successor should be fixed as appropriate for the office held, and not determined by the military rank held by the individual.[61]

Support from the Home Front

Inevitably, most priests were ill-prepared for what faced them and there was little by way of training or preparation. Most training was simply passed on from more experienced men to the new arrivals and immediate experience in the heat of battle was the most common form of training.[62] The tasks of the chaplains were supported by campaigns at home, including the pledge made by the Catholic weekly magazine, *The Tablet*, to provide every Catholic soldier with a 'devotional outfit', containing a Catholic prayer book, a pamphlet, rosary, scapular and Sacred Heart Badge.[63]

In June 1915, Parkinson made an optimistic and encouraging speech on the war 'from the Catholic point of view', to a meeting of the Catholic Women's League held at Oscott. He assured the gathering that the spiritual welfare of Catholic soldiers had never been so well looked after as in the present conflict, that a number of Oscotians were now serving in the ranks or as chaplains and that around 25,000 priests were serving among the armies of different countries. Unlike the British government, the governments of Europe, especially France, conscripted clergy, not only as chaplains but as combatants in the war. The British government exempted all clergy, and a parliamentary Bill to change this in 1918 failed to get support.[64]

A wartime official military Christmas card (Birmingham Archdiocesan Archives)

The CWL gathering at Oscott accidentally caused a sensation in the local press when George Turner, the owner of a taxi company transported ladies to the meeting from the parish of St Mary the Mount in nearby Walsall and found himself in court. It appears that insufficient taxis were provided, so that six ladies had to be pressed into the last vehicle, including one forced to kneel on the floor of the vehicle. *(His Honour: 'In an attitude of devotion?' Mr Wylie, the solicitor: 'Yes, compulsory devotion'.)* The taxi was driven at breakneck speed and on rounding a corner in Walsall, the door flew open and another passenger, Mrs Cecily Butler, was flung out on the road. The unfortunate lady suffered concussion and other injuries and took Mr Turner to court, claiming compensation for her injuries. A lengthy cross-examination led to Judge Howard dismissing Mrs Butler's claim.[65]

The Catholic chaplains were, on some occasions, actively supported in their work by some senior Catholic officers, such as Lt Col Rowland Feilding, commanding officer of the 6th Battalion, Connaught Rangers. The son of a Shropshire vicar, Feilding became a Catholic when he married Edith Stapleton-Bretherton, a Catholic, but he also had Catholic cousins, Rudolph and Everard who were educated at Oscott. They were the sons of Rudolph Feilding, 8th Earl of Denbigh, a convert to Catholicism and a generous benefactor to the Church in Wales. Rowland Feilding had previously served with the Coldstream Guards and was transferred to lead the Connaught Rangers, not only because of his experience in command, but because of his faith.

Feilding's *War Letters to a Wife*, first published in 1926 and in a new edition by Jonathan Walker in 2001, has been widely quoted by historians seeking to convey something of the real experiences of warfare. His letters frequently refer to the faith and practice of the soldiers. On Christmas Day 1916, following Mass celebrated for all those men able to attend (some 300), he remarked in a letter: 'The men manning the fire trench of course could not attend, but it was not a case of driving the rest – rather indeed of keeping them away. The intensity of their religion is something quite remarkable, and I had underestimated it'.[66]

Feilding's wife, Edith, with the help of Cardinal Bourne, obtained crucifixes for all his men, which the cardinal ensured had been blessed personally by Pope Benedict XV. With great solemnity, after Mass on 22 April 1917, the crucifixes were presented to the officers and men of the battalion. Feilding reported to his wife that she had 'a church full of soldiers, there must have been nearly a thousand altogether – straight from the battle line – praying for you this day'. He also reported that: 'One of my non-Catholic Company Commanders asked if he might take a crucifix. He told me later that it was the most impressive ceremony he had ever seen: and I may admit that the devout reverence of these soldiers, as they filed towards the altar, affected me too, very deeply'.[67]

Crucifixes, rosaries, holy medals and devotional pictures played a huge part in the soldiers' approach to life and preparation for death and the demand for them, among non-Catholics as well as Catholics, became almost impossible to fulfil. Whilst the likelihood of them being treated by some as talismans or good luck charms was real, so too was the need among the Catholic soldiers for devotional aids and familiar prayers and images as they faced the horrors of war. Fr Charles McDonnell, serving as chaplain with the 10th Battalion, Royal Dublin Fusiliers reported to Parkinson in early 1917: 'We have just had a spell of nine days in shell holes… The continued exposure has told its tale, but the men are quite wonderful in the way they take it. Every man recited his rosary in the shell holes regardless of any non-Catholics who were present'.[68]

British chaplain praying for a dying German soldier near Epehy, 18 September 1918 (Imperial War Museum Photograph Collection IWM Q 11336)

Fr Joseph Whitfield

The role of the Catholic chaplain in wartime became very immediate to the seminarians and staff at Oscott, when Fr Joseph Whitfield, Vice-Rector until June 1914, volunteered for service on the outbreak of war. Fr Stewart Foster, Archivist of the Diocese of Brentwood, provided the following biographical notes. Born in the East End of London to a Catholic family of part Jewish descent, Joseph Whitfield began his education at St Edmund's, Ware, completing a degree in Natural Sciences at St Edmund's House, Cambridge. In 1900 he entered Oscott to train for the priesthood and was ordained in September 1904. After ordination he was appointed to teach science and moral theology at St Edmund's, Ware. He was a gifted, perceptive and highly intelligent man who left a strong impression on Parkinson. In 1910 Parkinson asked the Archbishop of Birmingham to seek Whitfield's release from Westminster to become Vice-Rector at Oscott. Bourne consented and Whitfield returned to Oscott where he was later remembered for his 'rather forbidding appearance and old-fashioned ways.'

Fr Joseph Whitfield (Brentwood Diocesan Archives)

Fr Whitfield was one of the first wartime chaplaincy appointments, commissioned on 29 August 1914. By November he was attached to the Black Watch and in the same month crossed the Channel to Le Havre and served on HQ Staff 1st Infantry Division. By December 1914 he was attached to 1st Field Ambulance as part of 1st Infantry Division in Flanders. In March 1915, as chaplain to the 1st Cameron Highlanders, 1st Brigade, 1st Division with the BEF, he took the time to write a lengthy account of his life as a chaplain to his former students at Oscott, for publication in *The Oscotian Magazine*.

'But what is one out here for?'

Whitfield's letter carefully avoids any mention of location and takes a positive tone to comply with military regulations but is striking for its blend of vivid practical details of the discomforts and difficulties of life at the front and profound faith in the face of death.

When they were able to tell me where I was wanted, there was a two days journey in a supply train to be undertaken. The distance, indeed, could be covered in a car between lunch and teatime; but supply trains do not hurry. One comes up every day for each corps, and method is of more account than speed. The train consisted of about forty goods wagons and two first class coaches, one towards either end of the line of trucks. The one was for the colonel of the train – he spends his life aboard; the other was for those who, like myself, were going up. I had three gunners for company on the journey, two of whom had been wounded earlier in the campaign and were returning to duty, really glad to get back, though not without dread of the dangers.

When leaving the base I was quite in the dark as to my destination; when reaching railhead I knew nothing of which troops I should be attached to. I found then that my division was just coming down for a rest. It had borne the burden of the day since the beginning, and now after three months' hard work was to be relieved. And it needed it. I realised something of this on the next Sunday, when I had a mere sprinkling of a congregation from a whole brigade. It came down to a mere remnant of a brigade.

But the time of my joining was propitious. We rested for five weeks, and during that time I was able to get known to all the Catholics. I can't say that I knew them all, but they all knew me, and that is the more important. Well, week by week, my congregation grew, as new drafts came out, until they threatened to overflow the church. I made all arrangements for a general communion on Christmas Day, to be preceded by special preparation; sports and festivities were also arranged for that day – when suddenly, at very short notice, the brigade moved off on Sunday evening. For more than a month they were in the trenches by turn, and then they came down for four weeks' rest. Now we are up again.

The right place for chaplains to be centred in this method of warfare has been the subject of some discussion. My own experience inclines me to think that they should be attached to some regiment of their brigade. I was first attached to a field ambulance, with the consequence that, when my brigade was in the trenches, I was four miles behind and had to journey backwards and forwards day by day. When my brigade came down to rest, there were again some troops for whom I was responsible at a distance of four miles, while the nearest to me were two miles off. I am now attached to a regiment and live where my men are. Of course it is less comfortable, and, I suppose, more dangerous; but what is one out here for?

As at present arranged, half the brigade are in the trenches at a time, the rest being in reserve; they change over every two days. While they are in reserve I visit them in their billets and have an English service, after which I hear confessions. The next morning there is Mass and Holy Communion. All this is voluntary. On Sunday there is a parade service.

Until the present I have always had a church at my disposal, and I have ever found the *curés*, one and all, most cordial and generous in giving me all assistance in their power. Even when we were up, at the beginning of the year, we had a church close at hand, just behind our lines. The *curé's* house was wrecked, but he clung to the one room which remained with walls and ceiling intact though very waterstained. His church, when I first knew it, was unharmed and was beautifully kept, but one Saturday night it received some shells from the enemy, and from that time ceased to be the abode of the Blessed Sacrament – but the *curé* still uses his church. Where I am now there is no church, although there are many fine ones roundabout; but when troops are in reserve they cannot be marched a couple of miles for a church parade. I have found, however, a barn with plenty of good straw under foot, and until I am turned out, either by my own people, who may want it as a billet, or by the enemy, who may send a shell over some day, that will be my church.

It won't take in the whole congregation, but fine weather is here – to stay, I hope – and the farmyard makes an adequate annexe.

The work here is very full of consolations for a priest. The Cardinal said in his Pastoral that God had taken the work of Lenten missioners into his own hands this year. Here one sees much of the effectiveness of it. One hears confessions everywhere. Everyone knows what is going on and the penitent does not display the slightest self-consciousness, nor the non-Catholic spectator the slightest curiosity. Religion is all very real just now, and commands the respect even of those who were formerly the most indifferent. And God has his auxiliaries! When I arrive at a billet and call out 'Any R C's here?' I get a small knot about me, one of whom will start off to hunt up all the others and let them know of the priest's presence. As witness an incident – It was early in the year, a very cold day with an east wind, and I was up with the reserves. In a roofed-in structure, open at the sides and designed for stacking unthreshed corn, I was hearing confessions. Underfoot it was wet, the wind cut to the bone, and I was physically miserable. But scouting was being done for me, and there seemed no end to the quarry; so that after a time I had to put aside the hope, as each one came, that he might be the last. When the end did come I was thoroughly chilled and frozen, but unspeakably happy and most thankful to God for a good day's work done.

It appears to me that our soldiers are boys. In their sinning they are wilful but not malicious, and in their repentance they have all a boy's fervour and good will. One does not find a hardened sinner in a brigade; but one does see a strong and brave man in tears of sorrow, and the sight gives joy and pain. It was a great advantage to come straight from one's moral theology to this work – but principally from the point of view of sufficiency of the penitent's acts. This is the chaplain's principal work in the present warfare – confessing. Casualties are comparatively few, and serious ones may be called rare. If a man is wounded seriously unction at the front will only be possible if the chaplain is lucky. As soon as possible the wounded man is brought back to a dressing station. Since he is badly wounded he is sent down without delay by motor to an ambulance, thence to a clearing hospital, and so by hospital train to a base hospital. Only in those cases where an injury is almost certainly fatal will the chaplain at the front normally be able to anoint. Of course exceptions occur. It was the first night that I was under fire; I had been taken to all the dressing stations and shown my way round. Returning, I went to call somewhere, but failed to find the individual. But I sat down to talk and smoke. They told me that I had very few in that regiment and mentioned one name, which remained in my mind.

I passed on my way and came to the big house, where I was to await an ambulance to take me home. It was very cold, windows were broken, and there was no fire. There was, however, a piano, and two soldiers tried to entertain us with music and song, but as midnight approached, even that became a weariness. We had a man come in from the regiment I have referred to, and as he was a well-educated fellow we invited him to sit and share our accommodation. I was feeling intensely bored and wishing I had walked home instead of waiting for that car, when the car arrived. But it had picked up a case. The stretcher-bearer mentioned to the man of his regiment, who was with us, the name. It was the name that had been mentioned to me earlier in the evening. So I went down in the ambulance to the field hospital, and there anointed him after conditionally absolving. He had been hit at a dangerous part of the road when returning from his spell in the trenches, and was clearly fatally wounded. After I had left him, his identity disc was consulted, and it was found to give his religion as Presbyterian. So I was unable to bury him. But he was indeed a Catholic and a good one too, and as a result of someone's prayers he got the last sacraments in spite of the most unpromising circumstances. There was a good deal of slackness about identity discs in territorial regiments.

Funerals: where there is a cemetery we use it. Here there was none, and we have made one. Each grave is banked and turfed and the paths are made up of broken birch. It is very suitable and will doubtless prove permanent. At present each grave has a plain wooden cross. But this is the exception – normally we bury near the place of death. The military funeral is robbed of its bugles and firing party. Sometimes one has to bury by night, and say as much of the burial service as one knows by heart. I do feel that, for military funerals at least, a purely vernacular service would be more impressive.

Well, I might write to you much more, but must ask you to be content with this...

Yours sincerely,

J L Whitfield   17 March 1915

In 1917 Whitfield was serving with the 56th Division, and was twice Mentioned in Despatches from Field Marshal Sir Douglas Haig for gallant and distinguished services in the field in November 1917, and in March 1918 he was awarded the Distinguished Service Order. This was a relatively unusual decoration for a Chaplain to the Forces, but it was said that, had he not been a chaplain he would have been awarded the Victoria Cross. In later life, Whitfield was always reticent in speaking about the war and the circumstances surrounding his decoration, declaring that his medal had been received 'for not getting killed', and it was with difficulty that he was persuaded to attend the investiture by King George V at Buckingham Palace. It has been said that he had performed an act of great courage during the Battle of the Somme by entering no man's land under fire to rescue Captain Stuart Scarisbrick from certain death. In fact, this story was not quite accurate, although it passed into family tradition.[69]

Whitfield himself was wounded in action in 1917 and was invalided out of the army. He resigned his commission on 17 March 1918, leaving the army with a high reputation as a devoted chaplain. He entered the newly erected Diocese of Brentwood on 24 April 1918, but in June he was elected Master of St Edmund's House, Cambridge. After just over two years there, Whitfield returned to his diocese and a long and distinguished life of pastoral priesthood in Southend, whilst maintaining an active interest in Catholic history until his eyesight failed. He died in 1961.

Bombardier John Molloy

One of those 'auxiliaries' to whom Whitfield referred was John Molloy, who would have been well known to him as a student at Oscott, and was, from all accounts, a remarkable young man. Born on 6 May 1888, John Molloy went to Cotton College aged 14, where he proved to be a successful sportsman and a prize winning scholar. He entered Oscott in 1906 and showed the same aptitude, as well as social gifts in debating and singing and was described as 'brilliant, clever and witty, [and] a favourite with all he met'.[70] He abandoned thoughts of ordination and left in 1910, initially going into teaching in Weybridge, Surrey, but soon returning to his native Wolverhampton to take up a post in the engineer's office of the Great Western Railway. He enlisted under the short-lived voluntary Derby Scheme in 1915, and was called up in March 1916, going to France in July as a gunner in the Garrison Artillery.

Here, John Molloy's deep faith shaped his approach to the tasks he was called upon to perform. He never forgot that he had been a seminarian and often spoke of the chances of returning to his studies; he was fond of the Oscotian Society and always sought out those of his contemporaries who were priests.[71] John Molloy fulfilled an important pastoral role in the trenches, speaking readily of his faith and praying with and for the men around him, distributing prayer books and devotional

Philosophers' football team 25 October 1908. Those mentioned in the text are: William Bunce, tall figure standing at the back; Francis Lockett, standing, second from the right; Joseph Dwyer, seated on the end at the left; John Molloy is seated in the centre row to the right of the priest and seated on the ground in front of him is John Drinkwater the third of the Drinkwater brothers. (Birmingham Archdiocesan Archives)

objects and even preparing two French children for their first Holy Communion, according to the account given by Fr Francis Drinkwater, with whom he was in regular contact at the front. He described this as the happiest time he spent in France, and 'despite the hardships of the life he enjoyed his experiences immensely and would not have missed them for anything'.[72] Molloy's last pastoral action was to gather his companions together for Confession and Holy Communion, having met the chaplain by chance in the field. Nine days later he was killed instantly on 21 March 1918, aged 29.

One of the Oscotians who served as a chaplain, Fr William Bunce, had been a contemporary and friend of Molloy in the seminary and such was the chaos of war, he did not even know that his friend had been called up until he heard of his death. Bunce recalled that, 'to the superficial observer, his manner might have seemed somewhat careless and his tastes Bohemian, but the writer, who for years enjoyed his intimate companionship, will ever remember John Molloy as a faithful friend, a man of noble character, gifted with no mean talents. He had a generous heart, full of true, solid piety, ever maintaining, through a somewhat chequered career, a genuine devotion to Our Lady of Oscott'.[73] John Molloy has no known grave, and is commemorated in Bay 1 of the Arras Memorial, Pay de Calais. He is also commemorated on the Oscott war memorial. R I P.

Memorial to Bombardier John Molloy and other war victims with no known grave. (War Graves Photographic Project)

William Bunce himself was an exact contemporary of John Molloy, born in nearby Dudley and they were at Cotton College and Oscott together. He was not an outstanding student, but thorough in all he did. After leaving the army in 1920, he served in a number of parishes, but when he died suddenly of appendicitis, aged only 49, he was administrator of Father Hudson's Homes.[74] 'He had no enemies; he was a universal favourite; his hearty laugh and cheerful manner were infectious. He was just "big" Billie Bunce, to whom we looked up in more ways than one.'[75] That comment is borne out by the photograph of Bunce towering head and shoulders above his fellow students in an Oscott football team in 1908, see page 40.

Fr Herbert Collins

According to the records of *The Oscotian Magazine*, thirty Oscotian priests offered themselves for service as military chaplains during the war. Of these, seven, including Joseph Whitfield (later Brentwood), were from the Archdiocese of Westminster, four were from Salford, two from Southwark, one each from Newport, Clifton, Portsmouth and Edinburgh, and twelve from the Archdiocese of Birmingham. Fr Osmund Woods had been Whitfield's predecessor as Vice-Rector, but was not trained at Oscott. All of them except Fr Herbert Henry John Collins, a priest of the Archdiocese of Westminster, survived the war.

Herbert (Bertie) Collins was born in London on 27 December 1881, the son of James Thomas and Mary Campbell Collins and was a contemporary at St Edmund's, Ware and Oscott of Fr Joseph Whitfield and of Fr George Craven, both on active service as chaplains. Collins entered Oscott from St Edmund's in 1902, and was ordained on 12 July 1908. Widely admired and held in affection by all, Collins was good at study and games, 'the most joyous and bright spirit, friendly to all, and everyone's friend', in the words of Canon Burton, President of St Edmund's. Successful in studies, winning prizes, he had a good voice and was Dean of Students for his last 18 months at Oscott, and received a Gold Medal for good conduct. *The Oscotian*

Fr Herbert Collins was a highly successful student while at Oscott. (The Oscotian Magazine)

Magazine recorded that 'his spirit of loving cheerfulness has left a deep impression on the minds of his contemporaries'.[76]

After ordination Collins was appointed assistant priest at Brentford until June 1910, when he became assistant administrator of the Crusade of Rescue. He disliked office work, but threw himself into it. Cardinal Bourne, on hearing of Collins' death, said that many wondered why he had chosen Collins for this post, 'but very soon they came to realise no better choice could have been made.

I knew already his qualities, his cheerful devotion to duty, and his zeal for the salvation of souls, and I counted upon him to take a very great and leading part in the many works of charity that have grown up in the diocese...many a time during the past few months I thought of works to be entrusted to him on his return'. The Cardinal's plans were thwarted when Collins was killed by a shell on Easter Monday, 9th April 1917, while serving as chaplain to the Black Watch. According to the Adjutant of the Black Watch, 'his place can never be adequately filled'.

Herbert Collins' lifelong friend and Oscott classmate, Fr George Laurence Craven, was a Birmingham priest, who went on to be appointed Auxiliary Bishop in Westminster. Whilst in the trenches himself, he sent a poignant personal obituary of his friend to *The Oscotian Magazine*:

Herbert Collins was devoted to Oscott and proud of it. He volunteered in 1915 as a chaplain and had been with the Black Watch for two years; he was with them in the trenches and out, sharing their triumphs and hardships. He was with them from the Battle of Loos to the Battle of Arras, and from the Colonel to the serving boy he had friends who would gladly have given their lives to save his. The Colonel mourned his loss as he would a son or brother.

On the morning of the Battle of Arras, he took his stand at the regimental aid post with the doctor, the most advanced he could get, in order to be as near to the men as possible and ready to minister to the dying on the field. By 9.30, four hours after the infantry had advanced, the first objective had been taken, and the aid post was to be moved forward. The doctor and Collins went over the parapet together and got separated; within a few moments a shell exploded at his feet. By the time the doctor reached him he was dead. He was carried back to a house on the edge of Arras and was buried next day alongside a number of comrades.

The most striking thing about him was his cheeriness and sunny temperament that nothing could cloud. He was always cheery, never moody and however dull one felt, one always brightened on his approach. His happy nature and his intelligent lively humour won all hearts at once and held them gladly captive. Despite his war experiences he was never depressed or gloomy. The Colonel records how, for a week before Arras, they had lived in a wet, cold, miserable dugout, which depressed us all to the verge of suicide, all except the padre who kept us alive with his fun. He was simply wonderful. One night in a dugout in the Loos salient under heavy bombardment, he kept up everyone's spirits by singing comic songs.

His charm was more than superficial. Alongside the virtues of patience, humility and kindliness, he was entirely selfless. No man thought less of self. As a man and a priest he was far above the ordinary, which explains the remarkable hold that he had on all who knew him. His priestly life before the war was entirely given to others, with no thought for his own comfort or possessions. Whatever he had, he gave away, or left in friends' houses. It was the same when he joined the army. The delay in his salary coming through never exercised him. His last act before his death was to sink a considerable amount of his own money into a much needed canteen for his men, with no thought of whether he would get the money back. His unselfishness meant that he was always alongside the men in the forefront of fighting, which is how he died.

Students and staff working in the Oscott woods, April 1908. Herbert Collins is seated. (Birmingham Archdiocesan Archives)

Fr Craven's personal tribute to his friend serves as a fitting reminder of the cost of warfare and its lifelong legacy: 'While the war lasts we shall have little occasion to miss him: separation from one's friends and long silences on their part are of the things of the war; but when we return to our normal lives of which he formed so cherished a part, we shall find that even if our war losses number no more than his death, the sacrifice we have been called upon to make is no small one'. In a personal letter to Stephen Rawlinson, he remarked that Collins was 'an old and very dear friend of mine, and his death is a hard blow. His death, however, brings its own consolation, for it is not difficult to see in it reward for a life spent entirely and with complete devotion in Almighty God's service. He was a man as good as he was charming. That is saying a great deal.'[77]

Fr Herbert Collins had been recommended for the Military Cross in 1916, and was again commended for a posthumous honour. He lies in grave XVII.K10 in the Cabaret-Range British Cemetery at Sauchez, Pas de Calais and is commemorated on the Oscott memorial plaque. R I P.

Fr George Craven

That same Fr George Craven was a Birmingham priest, born in Wednesbury who was at Oscott from 1902 to 1908 with Collins, but not ordained until 1912, following studies at S. Sulpice in Paris. He was one of the first priests to put his name forward, just three days after war was declared.[78] He was equally briskly refused. Until 1915, when he volunteered again for chaplaincy service, this time successfully, he served at St Chad's Cathedral.

His experience in France illustrated the toll taken on chaplains in fulfilling their roles even when not on the battlefields. During 1916 Craven was posted to the Casualty Clearing Station at Bethune, which was under constant bombardment, forcing people to sleep in the cellars, and expecting to be moved at any moment.[79] After nine months living and working under terrible conditions, the local commanding officer wrote to Rawlinson himself recommending that Craven, whose health had been severely affected, be moved as soon as possible.

Colonel Hewetson admitted that he would be 'excessively sorry to lose him, as he has been most devoted to his duty', but insisted that, 'if he is to avoid a complete breakdown in his health, a complete change is desirable at once'.[80] The work of a chaplain in casualty clearing stations and field hospitals was horrific, as they constantly faced death and hideous injuries and as Craven pointed out, had to care for the staff as much, if not more, than the patients. Writing from the 14th General Hospital at Wimereux at the end of the same year, he urged Rawlinson to ensure the appointment of hospital chaplains 'for a lengthy period'. He made the important and perceptive point that patients moved through the medical system swiftly and were likely to be seen by a priest at some point, but the nurses and orderlies were dependent on the 'ordinary parish ministry' of the chaplain, and it was an important pastoral task for the chaplain to get to know them.[81]

In 1917 Craven was awarded the Military Cross. After the war he became very involved in the Crusade of Rescue in the Archdiocese of Westminster, perhaps taking up the role Cardinal Bourne had intended for Herbert Collins. Craven was responsible for the care of over 700 destitute children every year between 1920 and 1947, and was appointed an honorary Canon of Westminster. During these years he got to know Fr Bernard Griffin, who had a similar role with the Father Hudson's Society in Birmingham, and when Griffin was appointed Archbishop of Westminster in 1943, he asked for George Craven as his auxiliary bishop. After Griffin's death in 1956 and Cardinal Godfrey's death in 1963, Bishop Craven was responsible for the running of the Archdiocese during the *sede vacante*. Cardinal Heenan described him as 'the father of the diocese'. He died in 1967.

Sergeant Bartholomew Scanlon

As the 1914-18 conflict wore on, and more casualties and deaths were reported, *The Oscotian Magazine* began, from its December 1915 number, to publish a regular list of the dead and wounded associated with the College. Life in the seclusion of the seminary must have felt very strange for the young men gathered there, and there were clearly some who felt the call to war as much, if not more, than the call to priesthood. Among these was Bartholomew Scanlon, who paid the ultimate price. 'Bart' Scanlon was born on 4 November 1894, the son of Maurice Bartholomew Scanlon and Caroline Low Scanlon, of 53 St Paul's Rd, Manningham, Bradford, Yorks. He was a schoolboy at Cotton College for seven years before entering Oscott to train for the priesthood in September 1914. An average scholar with a bent for mathematics, carrying off all the prizes in that subject, he had a

Sgt Bartholomew Scanlon was just 21 when killed on 30 January 1916. (War Graves Photographic Project)

reputation for tenacity of purpose and doggedness. Not a sportsman by nature, he despised training and preparation, yet was often capable of winning unexpectedly. After only a few months at Oscott, Scanlon volunteered for the army, leaving in April 1915 to join the 5th Cameron Highlanders, achieving rapid promotion to sergeant and training as a scout. This was one of the most exposed tasks in the trenches and Bart Scanlon was shot at a listening post and died instantly on 30 January 1916, aged 21. The chaplain serving with the Black Watch, Fr John McNeill, wrote to Parkinson the following day:

A recent pupil of yours, Sergeant B C Scanlon, was, unfortunately killed last night when in charge of a party at a listening post. I knew his history, as did his commanding officer, who was very fond of him, and respected him. He only joined this battalion out here in October last, and he had already been promoted to Sergeant, and would certainly have been able to secure a commission. He made his confession to me only on Saturday last, while both of us sat on a sandbag in the fire trench. An exemplary lad and a good soldier, I think you will be glad to count him among the college's honoured sons. RIP.

His commanding officer said that he 'died while doing his duty conscientiously, exposing himself fearlessly at his post so as the more thoroughly to safeguard the rest'. He paid tribute to his courage and efficiency: 'always alert, always reliable, and extremely capable, he was an example to the whole company'. Sergeant Bartholomew Scanlon lies in grave C 15 Hyde Park Corner (Royal Berks) Cemetery, Hainault, Belgium and is commemorated on the Oscott war memorial. R I P.

1 Hyde Park Corner Royal Berks Cemetery, Hainault, Belgium, holds the grave of Sergeant Bart Scanlon.

British chaplain decorating an altar with flowers in his church hut at Sailly-Labourse, 4 July 1918 (Imperial War Museum Photograph Collection IWM Q 11041)

Cardinal Bourne receiving chaplains of 16th Irish Division at Ervilles, 27 October 1917 (Imperial War Museum Photograph Collection IWM Q 6143)

Mgr James Dey, Rector of Oscott College 1929-1935 (Oscott College)

Left: Fr Francis H. Drinkwater (Museum of Army Chaplaincy)

Below: War medals and decorations including the CBE and DSO won by Mgr Charles Smith, Principal Catholic Chaplain (Museum of Army Chaplaincy)

Very Rev MGR C W Smith CBE, DSO

Commander of the British Empire, Distinguished Service Order, 1914-15 Star, 1914-20 War Medal, 1914-18 Victory Medal with Mention

Principal Roman Catholic Chaplain

Mgr Henry Parkinson, Rector of Oscott College 1896-1924. (Oscott College)

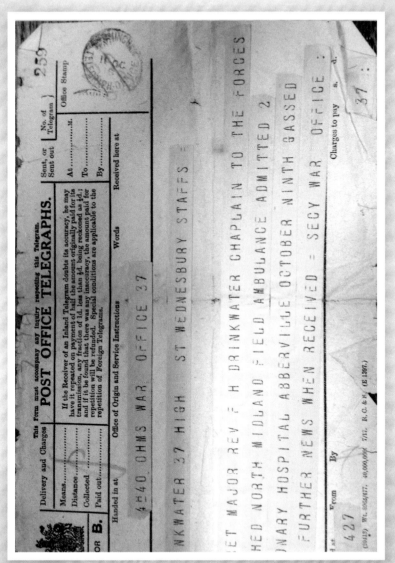

Telegram to Fr Francis H. Drinkwater's family, informing them of his injury in a gas attack (Birmingham Archdiocesan Archives)

Grave of Fr Herbert Collins at Cabaret-Rouge British Cemetery, Souchez, Pas de Calais. He was the only Oscotian chaplain killed during the war. (War Graves Photographic Project)

Rev G L Craven MC

Military Cross, 1914-15 Star, 1914-20 War Medal, 1914-18 Victory Medal with Mention

Above: *Basra Military Cemetery in modern day Iraq, the burial place of Lt Col Thomas Britten. (War Graves Photographic Project)*

Left: *Medals won by Fr George Craven while serving as a military chaplain. He was later appointed an Auxiliary Bishop in Westminster. (Museum of Army Chaplaincy)*

Left: The chapel at Oscott (Oscott College)

Below left: Archbishop Thomas Williams (courtesy the Archbishop of Birmingham)

Below right: Fr Philip Rhodes who taught theology and became Prefect of Studies at Oscott was a noted scholar and a respected botanist. (courtesy the Archbishop of Birmingham)

War Privations at Oscott

By the winter of 1915-16, the privations on the domestic front were beginning to bite and seminary life held little cheer. The little local excitements that punctuated life at Oscott were recorded with relish, such as the unexpected descent of a biplane out of the fog onto the field below the observatory. A learner pilot from the airfield at Castle Bromwich got into difficulties and had to make an emergency landing. A message was sent to Castle Bromwich and two officers and a mechanic arrived. 'One of the officers got into the biplane, it was not long before the machine rose gracefully from the rising ground, towards the bathing pool, then turned and was soon lost in the fog as it flew swiftly homewards'.[82]

New lighting regulations in February 1916 required blackout curtains to be fitted on all dormitory windows. The absence of curtains suggests living conditions at Oscott were spartan, even without wartime restrictions. The makeshift curtains were not of uniform shape or colour, but served the purpose. Only one gas lamp, placed near the pulpit, was permitted in chapel for night prayers and services were adapted as necessary. No Tuesday Compline was said in chapel and Thursday Benediction took place at 7.10 instead of after night prayer. In the same month supplies of coke for heating finally ran out and the hot water pipes were sealed off. The diarist in *The Oscotian Magazine* commented that, as the ground was covered with snow, a Common Room fire was but poor compensation for the loss of heating throughout building. That March, perhaps to remind the seminary of the real cost of war, the Rector began the celebration of a monthly requiem Mass for all those killed in the conflict.

Conscription and the Issue
of Exemption

The Military Service Act, which conscripted all able-bodied single men aged between eighteen and forty five into active service, came into force on 2 March 1916. Later in the year it was amended to include married men and in 1918 the upper age limit was raised to fifty one. Clergy of all denominations were exempt under the Act and conscription was not attempted in Ireland due to the fragile political relationship between the Irish Nationalists and the British government. Cardinal Bourne's negotiations with the War Office over the winter of 1915-16 had secured the exemption of men who had received Holy Orders (subdeacon, deacon or priest), by a quietly negotiated administrative order, rather than pressing for legislative exemption through Parliament, which could have raised public hackles,[83] but seminarians were still vulnerable until clarity could be ensured.

There was a suggestion made that all seminary students might join the Royal Army Medical Corps, if they gained exemption from combatant service, but in January 1916 the RAMC had sufficient recruits and had, for the time being, closed its books. Cardinal Bourne was advised that seminarians should appeal as a body to local conscription tribunals to be placed in a category to await further recruitment by the RAMC, but this apparently came to naught.[84] It still left uncertainty as to whether seminarians had to present themselves at local tribunals to gain release from conscription.[85] The War Office itself appeared unclear, suggesting vaguely that 'they probably would be dispensed from presenting themselves', but it was 'being pestered by nonconformists and others', and it was possible that the matter would go before Parliament, so the War Office was treading cautiously. Mgr Jackman, at Archbishop's House, Westminster, was sanguine that 'they will keep their faith absolutely to the bishops, and our men are quite safe'.[86] His confidence was ill-founded.

The terms of the clerical exemption still left seminarians in an insecure position when conscription was extended later in the year and in early 1917, Mgr Manuel Bidwell at Archbishop's House, Westminster wrote to Ilsley to tell him that the War

Office proposed to call up all theological students who were not members of religious orders. They would be given a month's notice and the right of appeal to a tribunal. He had argued, to no avail, that the existing exemption was agreed between the bishops and the previous government[87] and that the same reasons still applied. Bourne was on a prolonged visit to Rome but Bidwell urged the other bishops not to wait for his return, and to meet to discuss this as a matter of urgency.[88]

Not everyone shared Bidwell's sense of urgency. Archbishop Whiteside of Liverpool declared himself 'not too worried' because there was 'an honourable understanding with the government'. He did, however, begin to identify the problem by distinguishing between 'excepted' men, who were already in seminary when the administrative order was agreed between the bishops and the War Office, who could not be touched by tribunals, and 'exempted' men, who applied to tribunals as individuals in order to begin seminary. Whiteside suggested that Cardinal Bourne was hesitant in supporting these men, in case it jeopardised the position of those 'excepted' under the existing agreement.[89] This was certainly an issue, as a later case in Birmingham illustrated. Fr Edward Pereira, head of the Birmingham Oratory School, asked Ilsley's guidance in the case of Philip Rhodes, a highly gifted and devout lay master and former Anglican clergyman. He wished to pursue studies for the priesthood but the military authorities warned that if he resigned his teaching post to enter seminary, he would immediately become liable to be called up.[90]

Conscious of his direct responsibility for the men at Oscott threatened by conscription, in Bourne's absence Ilsley took Bidwell's advice and called the bishops together in March 1917. Parkinson was determined to ensure that seminarians remained in formation at Oscott if that was their wish. In March 1917 he set up an allowance at Oscott that provided for seminarians who were called up, creating the option of replacing a conscripted seminarian with a priest from his diocese who would then serve as a chaplain.[91] This became the key to the national solution negotiated with the War Office. The minutes of the bishops' meeting in March show that they, and the absent cardinal, had reached what they called the 'chaplain substitute compromise'. Any student who was due to be a subdeacon (so in orders) by the end of 1917 would be exempt from conscription if a chaplain could be supplied to substitute for him by the end of the year.[92] This compromise solution applied equally to students currently in the English Colleges in Rome, Spain, Portugal and elsewhere in Europe, as well as those on home territory.[93] By 1918, the 150 or so seminarians at risk of conscription were roughly

When he was called up, College gardener Henry Benedict Bullivent was fortunate not to be sent to the trenches but served in the Labour Corps. (The Bullivent family)

Henry Jackson, the long-serving butler at Oscott (The Oscotian Magazine)

equivalent to the shortfall of Catholic chaplains and it was expected that, after ordination, they either became chaplains or replace a priest in their diocese freed to do chaplaincy work.[94]

By the end of 1916, virtually all the ground staff at Oscott, who kept the seminary fed, especially during wartime shortages, had either volunteered or been called up. Among them was Henry Bullivent, who worked in the gardens, while his wife Emily worked in the kitchen. When Henry was called up in November 1916, he was not sent to the trenches, but to the Labour Corps, which suggests that his health was less than the 'A1' required for front line troops. Ironically, it was the Labour Corps that did much of the manual work in maintaining communications and infrastructure, both in areas of fighting and at home. Henry was sent to work, probably in much needed agriculture in Wiltshire, but in 1918, he was invalided out, due to his poor health.

After the war, Henry continued to work in the gardens at Oscott and lived with Emily first in the south lodge, later moving into the north lodge. Henry died in 1959 and Emily in 1963 and both were buried in the staff section of the College cemetery.[95]

Students volunteered to work in the grounds, in the absence of gardeners and some help was obtained from soldiers convalescing at a camp in Sutton Park. When they were recalled, the students had to do more outdoor manual work, so the Rector moved afternoon lectures to evenings, to make full use of daylight. Despite the hardships, some semblance of normal life was kept up. On 30 May 1917 the College celebrated 50 years of service by 'Henry' Jackson, the devoted College butler. His name was really William but he had been called Henry as an under butler, to avoid confusion with the previous head butler who was also William. His four

Lt Col William Dugmore was killed on 12 June 1917 and lies in Railway Dugouts Burial Ground, West Vlaanderen, Belgium. (War Graves Photographic Project)

sons, including Joe, previously the College's under butler, were all on active service. One had been killed, one invalided out and two were still serving by this time. William himself died on 25 November 1925, aged 75 after 58 years' service at Oscott and is buried in the College staff section of the Oscott cemetery.

The summer of 1917 also saw the death of another distinguished Oscotian military commander, Lt. Col. William Francis Brougham Radcliffe Dugmore DSO, the eldest son of the late Captain Francis Sandys Dugmore and grandson of 2nd Baron Brougham and Vaux, so a member of one of the oldest Catholic Recusant families. He was at Oscott from 1881 to 1883 and returned in February 1885 until midsummer of the following year. He joined the regular army, was commissioned in the 17th Lancers, made Captain in 1901 and retired eight years later. Captain Dugmore was Mentioned in Despatches and received the DSO for action in Africa. Further decorations from the Boer War (Queen's medal) and East Africa followed, and he was Mentioned in Despatches in the 1914-18 War. On 12 June 1917 he was killed in action while serving with the North Staffordshire Regiment, aged 49. Lt. Col. William Dugmore lies in grave VII.N.1 Railway Dugouts Burial Ground (Transport Farm) West Vlaanderen, Belgium and is commemorated on the Oscott war memorial. R I P.

The Drinkwater Brothers

Also during the summer of 1917, Oscott noted the commission given to one of two brothers, both Oscotians, one of whom was ordained and served as a chaplain while the other left Oscott to join up and was commissioned into the Royal Flying Corps. Fl. Lt Edward Oscar Drinkwater was probably the first Oscotian in history to take to the skies. The two brothers, Edward Oscar (known to his family and friends as 'Oxo') and Francis Harold, along with a third brother, John, were all seminarians at Oscott. Oscar entered as war broke out, in September 1914, by which time his brothers Francis and John had been ordained for several years. Francis Drinkwater survived serious shrapnel wounds and a gas attack which temporarily blinded him and served as a military chaplain through to 1919. The diary he kept of his wartime career is one of the fullest of wartime diaries, in which he records much time spent seeking out Catholic soldiers, while unattached to a particular regiment. Very often he recounts frustrating occasions of planning and setting up for Mass, only to find that the arrangements had not been communicated to the men by preoccupied military officers, or to find that battalions were moved at short notice and the men had left the area.

Oscar Drinkwater began his education at St Philip's Grammar School, adjoining the Birmingham Oratory, and then passed to Cotton College as a Church student. He left in 1911 for Angers in France to study Philosophy but the outbreak of war meant a hasty return and his studies resumed at Oscott. He distinguished himself in every sphere, was well above average in studies and an energetic and skilful sportsman. Able to enthuse other students with his passion for golf, he built a bunker in a neglected flower garden. He became a member of all College societies and was very public spirited. No office was

Fl. Lt Oscar Drinkwater was probably the first Oscotian aviator. (Birmingham Archdiocesan Archives)

too burdensome; all that were offered to him were willingly accepted and reliably and generously carried out, without expectation of gratitude. 'As a social unit Oscar had a peculiar charm.' He had an even and easy temper, a contemplative turn of mind, an engaging and peaceable disposition, displaying simplicity and candour.

Although Oscar was thriving at Oscott, he was already beginning to question his vocation and after several requests to be allowed to join up, he finally left seminary permanently. He married Ruby Moore soon after and set up home in Maidenhead, where a daughter was born in April 1918. In February 1917 he joined the King's Own Rifles but transferred to the Royal Flying Corps. This was the overland air arm of the British army during most of the First World War. During the early part of the war, the RFC's responsibilities were centred on support of the British army, via artillery co-operation and photographic reconnaissance. Four aeroplane squadrons were first used for aerial spotting on 13 September 1914, but only became efficient when they perfected the use of wireless communication at Aubers Ridge on 9 May 1915. Aerial photography was attempted during 1914, but only became effective in the following year. Parachutes were not available to the pilots of the RFC's heavier than normal aircraft, so any attack on a reconnaissance plane meant almost certain death. Fl. Lt Oscar Drinkwater was involved in this dangerous work from May 1918.

Oscar's brother, Francis, records in his diary that in August 1917 his brother joined the RFC, getting his wings in March 1918. He left for France in May and the two brothers met up in Bethune. Aged only 23, Oscar became the star reconnaissance photographer, working in great danger over German lines before La Bassée, often going out two or three times a day. On 23 August 1918 he was flying at 6,000 feet when his plane was hit by a shell and corkscrewed to the ground. A couple of days later Francis Drinkwater questioned a German prisoner of war who saw the crash and told him that in its last descent the plane had nosedived, giving no hope of survival. When the plane was found, local people spoke of the pilot being carried away unconscious. Only later was he confirmed dead and buried in an unmarked grave at Auchy.

Many years later, in 1979, Francis Drinkwater revisited his wartime diary and filled in some details, including this description of his brother's fate. Some months after the Armistice, returning to the area where Oscar's plane went down and aided by the photographs Oscar himself had taken along with accounts from local people, Francis located his unmarked grave. He was still able to identify the remains as those of his brother: 'just a few fragmented bones really'. A local man gave him his shirt in which he carefully wrapped the bones and returned to his hotel room with them. He spent the night in prayer, washing them, initially determined to take them home for a family funeral. On considering the complexity in the immediate post-war months of repatriating the human remains of a military officer, he reluctantly resolved to leave the task in the hands of the Imperial (later Commonwealth) War Graves Commission, which ensured burial in France with military honours.[96] Fl. Lt Edward Oscar Drinkwater lies in grave VIII.H.10, Brown's Road Military Cemetery, Festubert, Pas de Calais, and is commemorated on the Oscott war memorial. R I P.

The last resting place of Fl. Lt Oscar Drinkwater, Brown's Road Military Cemetery, Calais (War Graves Photographic Project)

Fr Francis H. Drinkwater

Francis Drinkwater lived to a great age, dying in 1982, having devoted his priestly ministry to catechesis for young people through his children's plays and stories and through the creation and publication of *The Sower*, a vehicle for spreading his fresh and challenging approach to catechesis. In a memoir of Drinkwater, his contemporary at Oscott, Mgr James Crichton drily remarked: 'I think one may fairly call it a *Sower* principle that it is against God's will to bore people with religion.'[97]

The seeds of this work were sown even before the war when Drinkwater was curate to William Barry at Leamington Spa and worked in the schools there. Barry commented that Drinkwater had the finest mind he had met among the young men of the diocese.[98] Drinkwater's wartime experience of seeing so many young Catholic boys going to their deaths with little understanding of their faith or of God's unfailing love for each one of them resonated with his pre-war catechetical work and shaped the rest of his life.

This struck him very early in the war, as he recorded in his diary on 12 August 1915: 'Wrote a letter to Fr. Pritchard; I congratulated him on his booklet guide to the Mass, and said we were making good Catholics out of bad ones by the score here; could he think of any way of keeping them up to it on their return, and write an article in *The Tablet* about it?' Similar thoughts would be stirred by exchanges such as this, with one of his soldier penitents: '16 September: "When was your last confession" "The last war, father".' He had an ear for the bleak humour of the soldiers, recording an exchange on 10 August 1915: 'One man said, "It's rather a bad time for you gentlemen, isn't it sir? Difficult to believe in Almighty God with all this going on". However, he was very cheerful, and we parted friends.'[99]

Drinkwater's letters to his family and his diary evoke much of the atmosphere of the trenches, as he described it to his sister, Agnes, in a letter of 13 August 1916: 'I said Mass at two places this morning, one at 10.30, then off to another place for 11.30. It was all quiet there too, except for two or three stray bullets that wandered around the place where I was saying Mass. The church there is destroyed and they use a sort of barn place fitted up with altar etc. In our own village we don't get any bullets, even at night when the machine guns are active, because we are in a hollow. You can see the German trenches easily enough from the rising ground behind, but I have never managed to see a German.'[100] Rawlinson was unstinting in his admiration for Drinkwater: 'He is really a splendid man, and has done first rate work out here for the past three years and a half'.[101]

A French church after bombardment (Birmingham Archdiocesan Archives)

Lt Col Victor Mottet de la Fontaine

Also lost in 1917 was another of Oscott's regular soldiers and one of the six Oscotian war dead who received the DSO.[102] Lt Col Victor Mottet de la Fontaine was killed in action on 5 August after nearly two years' service in command of a battalion of the East Surrey Regiment. He was educated at Oscott 1871-5 and again 1886-9, a timid boy, whose grit and determination made him into a fearless and brave officer. His sense of duty was one of his strongest characteristics. He was an exemplary son and brother and always considerate for others. His moral stature and piety were evident. One comrade described him as 'a very perfect gentleman, more like a crusader of old than a present day man of the world. I feel he was such a saint and yet such a real man that it did me good to know him'.[103]

The grave of Lt Col Victor de la Fontaine, killed by a sniper on 5 August 1917 (War Graves Photographic Project)

De la Fontaine was a qualified interpreter and served in South Africa, twice being Mentioned in Despatches and wounded going to the rescue of a fellow officer. In June 1911 he became a Major in the East Surrey Regiment. After the battle of Loos in autumn 1915 he was made Lt Col of a battalion, making himself loved and respected by men in all ranks, instilling in them 'that human nature and discipline…which alone can come from a sincere friend'. He commanded his battalion with conspicuous gallantry and devotion until his death. His battalion was nearly destroyed in successive attacks, in the last of which he was seriously wounded and awarded the DSO.

On the morning of 5 August 1917 some of the advance posts had been attacked and it was necessary to assess the situation. He went himself, rather than sending a junior officer and on his return journey was shot dead by a sniper. He had received absolution from the chaplain of the 72nd Brigade just before he went up the line for the last time. According to a Captain of the East Surreys: 'His death has robbed the battalion of a noble and fearless leader, a gallant gentleman and a true friend'.

Fr Stafford, Senior Chaplain of his division wrote: 'He was something more than a favourite with both officers and men; they looked up to him as a soldier and a man, and his high moral tone no less than his heroic courage was acknowledged on all sides.' His Brigadier General wrote to his parents: 'Your son was one of the most gallant and fearless soldiers I have met in this European War and absolutely without regard for himself when duty called him'. Lt Col Victor Mottet de la Fontaine lies in grave III.C.15 Reninghelst New Military Cemetery, West Vlaanderen, Belgium, and is commemorated on the Oscott war memorial. R I P.

Oscott Reaches its Lowest Ebb

The loss of so many Oscotian friends and brothers in 1917, combined with the increasing shortages of basic supplies, began to cast a gloom over life in the seminary, as in the wider population. Food shortages were a feature of life everywhere and the difficulties of securing supplies of wheat meant that the depleted supplies of staple foods including bread were rising in price. The government ruled that millers could not mill pure wheat flour but had to adulterate it with 5-10% barley, oats, rye, etc, provoking the bishops to ask for assurances on the accessibility of pure wheat flour for the manufacture of altar breads.[104] In March 1917 Frank Wells, who worked the College Farm at Oscott, was among a number of local farmers brought to court and fined (£100) for selling potatoes at a price above that fixed by the government.[105] This meant that Christmas 1917 was a dismal affair in the seminary. The College diary recorded for 25 December: 'On Christmas Day only Low Masses were celebrated. The Rector and Vice-Rector were the only two at dinner and there was no turkey or plum pudding'.

All the students were now expected to work outside to maintain the farm and gardens and morale raising house concerts were becoming impossible, given the small number of students in residence. Oscott, like the rest of the nation, began the new year of 1918 in low spirits. For the first time, in the summer of 1918, no Oscotian Day was celebrated, reflecting both the sombre mood and the wartime shortage of supplies.

Early in the year the melancholy mood was reflected in the reporting of the death of the Hon. Edward Noel, who had been a schoolboy at Oscott in the 1860s. His military career was behind him and his life was devoted to his three sons and the practice of his faith. He was a very reserved and deeply religious man who spoke little, except of God, and was often to be seen making the Stations of the Cross early each morning in the Carmelite church in west London. His schoolboy friend from Oscott days, Arthur Ryan, now a serving chaplain in the war, wrote movingly of their last meeting when they had talked long into the night, recalling affectionate memories of their happy schooldays at Oscott, and a world long gone forever: 'And so we chatted on, two old men turned boys again over the mid-winter fire, until the time came for what was to be our last goodnight, he to return to his war work in the censor's office, I to take my turn as chaplain at the front, both trying to do our bit in the awful times in which we had lived.'[106]

Final Oscotian Deaths

The last Oscotian deaths of the First World War commemorated on the College's memorial plaque were not men distinguished by high military rank or awards for gallantry. They represent, perhaps more fittingly, the millions of men whose stories are unrecorded, the ordinary 'Tommies'. These men are exemplified by Private Leo Thomas Bernard Kelly, who was born in Heath Town, Wolverhampton in 1889, one of two children of Catherine and James Kelly, who was an Irish born policeman. Leo entered Oscott on 16 September 1908, but only stayed one year. After Oscott, he is recorded in the 1911 Census as living in Holly Lane, Erdington as an assistant schoolmaster. Nothing else is known of him except that he was killed in action with

Private Leo Kelly served with the Household Cavalry and was killed on 1 April 1918.
(War Graves Photographic Project)

the 20th Hussars Battalion of the Household Cavalry on 1 April 1918. His family home is then recorded as Stone, Staffordshire. Private Leo Kelly has no known grave, but is commemorated on panel 6 of the Poziers Memorial in the district of the Somme. According to information from the Commonwealth War Graves Commission, this memorial relates to the period of crisis in March and April 1918 when the Allied Fifth Army was driven back by overwhelming numbers across the former Somme battlefields and the months that followed before the advance to victory, which began on 8 August 1918. The memorial commemorates over 14,000 casualties of the United Kingdom and 300 of the South African forces who have no known grave and who died on the Somme between 21 March and 7 August 1918. Private Leo Kelly, although an Oscotian only for one year and whose story is lost, is commemorated on the Oscott war memorial. R I P.

Lieutenant Joseph Arnold

Joseph Arnold was born in St Helens and educated at Cotton College between 1897 and 1903. In 1903 he entered Oscott as a student for the Archdiocese of Liverpool but left after summer 1905. He went into teaching at St Joseph's Boys' School in Leeds. In May 1915 he entered the Manchester Regiment as a Private, was made Corporal the following July and Sergeant in February 1916. After four months in France, Arnold was recommended for a commission, which he received in May 1917. Two months later he returned to France with his old regiment and only a week after returning from leave was killed by machine gun fire while leading his platoon in the storming of Villers-au-Flos on 2 September 1918. He left a widow, Marie who lived in Leeds and a two year old son, Joseph. She reported to Parkinson that the chaplain who was present at his burial,

Lt Joseph Arnold was killed by machine gun fire at Villers-au-Flos on 2 September 1918.

Fr McGinnell from Salford Diocese, had visited her and she asked that Parkinson inform Fr Charles McDonnell, another Oscotian chaplain, as her husband and he were old school friends.[107] At the Memorial Mass held in Leeds, 800 schoolchildren attended from the school where Joseph Arnold had taught for 15 years. Lt Joseph Arnold lies in grave B8, Manchester Cemetery, Riencourt-les-Bapaume Cemetery, Pas de Calais and is commemorated on the Oscott war memorial. R I P.

Lance Corporal John Stokes

The last Oscotian of all to fall in the 1914-18 war was John Stokes, a student for the Diocese of Menevia, although his war record gives his place of birth as Warrington, Lancashire and a surviving brother was recorded as living there. Born in 1894, he entered Oscott in October 1916 but remained only two months. As far as it is possible to ascertain he joined the Royal Dublin Fusiliers and in April 1917 asked Parkinson for a reference in order to apply for a commission.

Despite his brief knowledge of John Stokes, Parkinson sent a short but positive commendation, for which Stokes expressed his gratitude with all the optimism of youth: 'I have no doubt about its efficacy in producing the desired result.'[108] Lance Corporal John Stokes (listed as Private according to the official Irish War Dead List) died of wounds on 8 October 1918 and lies in grave III.B.10 in Prospect Hill Cemetery, Gouy, Aisne, France. Like Private Leo Kelly, his story is lost but he is commemorated on the Oscott war memorial and is prayed for as an Oscotian of the briefest possible duration whose life was cut short. R I P

Letter from John Stokes requesting a reference so he could apply for a commission. (Birmingham Archdiocesan Archives)

Lance Corporal John Stokes was the last Oscotian to be killed in the First World War. (War Graves Photographic Project)

The Morale of the Chaplains

Even in the last months of the war the conditions under which the chaplains operated were as difficult as ever and letters to Parkinson from the Front contain comments about the shortage of chaplains and the hardships, such as travelling under treacherous circumstances to say Mass in distant locations whilst maintaining the Eucharistic fast before Mass. The Church lifted the requirement of fasting in wartime conditions for the serving men but not for the chaplains.[109] This meant that priests were doing long journeys, often on foot, to celebrate two or more Masses in a day, without breaking their fast. It was a serious enough question to be taken up at a formal level by Fr James Dey, in correspondence with Rawlinson. His sympathetic response, too late to have any effect before the war ended, reveals much about the conditions of chaplaincy life in the last months of the war, torn between the authority of the Church and of the army and the needs of the Catholic soldiers.

Soldiers of 57th Brigade, 19th Division, attending Mass in the ruins of Cambrai Cathedral, 13 October 1918 (Fr E. Rockliffe SJ, Imperial War Museum Photograph collection IWM Q9548)

I note that the bishop does not feel inclined to ask for any special privileges with regard to the question of fasting until he is more convinced than at present of the need for them. I do not know if any words of mine can help in any way. Personally I am fully convinced that it would assist to a very high degree the work and efficiency of the chaplains in the field. Although it may be true, 'that some chaplains at times are less inclined than perhaps they should be, to suffer occasional hardships in the execution of their duty' I hardly think that this accusation could be made against more than say 5% of those out here. And it is not from such men that the application for saying Mass non-fasting has ever come. The men whom I would plead for are the other 95% many of whom are suffering from the strain of three or more years constant work in the front line, their nerves racked with gunfire by day and bombs by night, and who are called upon to say two Masses every Sunday for units a considerable distance apart, and generally without proper means of transport if any. It is from these most self-sacrificing and zealous priests only that the desire for a dispensation has come very frequently during the last two years, and never from one of the few would-be drones. It must not be forgotten that many priests have been in the front line for three or four years uncomplaining, who would certainly have had well merited rests at the Base, had the shortage of priests out here not prevented it. Three hundred men are doing the work of four hundred. I would, therefore, strongly recommend that the dispensation be obtained if possible, and I feel sure it will prevent the breaking down and casualties in our ranks which we can ill afford.[110]

Fr George Ayles-Waters of Salford Diocese told Parkinson, with robust humour, of the trials of everyday life: he reported that he was 'at present *curé* of a village church, such as in future days I might hope to obtain. The church is sadly out of repair, looks inside as if an earthquake had shaken it. It seems to bear a charmed life, every day I marvel to see it still in position. I dare not keep the Blessed Sacrament there, but carry it away. Daily I say Mass and give Benediction, despite the obvious difficulties. The organ will not play again, although I have two organists – t'would puzzle them to get a tune out of it. Further up towards the line I said Mass in a glorious church, which is heavily shelled. I told the men they were not obliged to hear Mass. They came and crowded it out and used up a whole cardboard box of communion hosts'.[111] It was obvious from all the chaplains' correspondence that it was the expressions of faith among the soldiers that kept the priests going through the horrors and discomforts.

The practical difficulties of obtaining, transporting and resupplying all that a priest needed to celebrate the sacraments were considerable. Transport was difficult to get, horses could be requisitioned, bicycles of little use in a war-torn landscape, and a priest would be carrying vestments, an altar stone, candlesticks, wine and hosts and even a set of hymnbooks.[112] Fr Charles McDonnell was anxious, as soon as his appointment was confirmed, to ascertain whether he had to find himself supplies of hosts and wine, or whether they would be supplied for him.[113] Ayles-Waters wrote lightheartedly about problems such as the considerable difficulty of obtaining altar wine, as so few French clergy were still in residence to supply any, but how ordinary wine, which seemed readily available, was used as

Fr George Ayles-Waters and his brothers (Museum of Army Chaplaincy)

an alternative. He delighted in the challenge he had set himself of making one convert for every Catholic he buried, 'as I think it lawful that our manpower should not suffer. I was one behind on Saturday, but another has walked into my claws, so I can be square again… Can you picture instruction [in the faith] in a dugout not high enough to stand upright, with shellholes all around and shrapnel bursting on the plain. Baptism with a water bottle, to be followed by Communion?'[114]

Yet beyond the bluff humour, it was clear that by the early summer of 1918 it was becoming harder for chaplains to keep up their own spirits. 'The war is taking a heavy toll of us now; numerous students [from Oscott] have fallen. The post the other day brought news of the death of four more chaplains. We were told at the last conference that those of us still alive by August could consider ourselves very lucky. He [the senior chaplain] wanted us to act less like daredevils, attempting to lead men etc. PS If anything happens to me, you will remember I am an Oscotian and put me on the college list, will you not?'[115]

Chaplains were faced with situations in which, as the war ground to its bitter end, fruitless attacks intensified, and they were as much in demand by the local population as by the serving soldiers. One report from the last days of the war spoke of the suffering of hundreds of poor people 'dying without a priest and being buried without religious rites. They arrive here, evacuated from villages, worn, weary, homeless and helpless, and in this "city of refuge" they are shelled, bombed and gassed. I have had twenty deaths within a few days. In nearly four years in France I have not seen more intense suffering or greater misery'.[116]

Naturally enough, as the war dragged towards its conclusion chaplains began to look tentatively to the future, although as Ayles-Waters reflected: 'The future seems clouded with anxiety everywhere.'[117] He had his own personal anxieties about the future, having met and fallen in love with a nurse, Edith Wadsworth, while in France. When he was demobilised in 1922, Ayles-Waters returned to active priestly ministry in his diocese, as curate at St Mary's Oldham, but he was, it must be presumed, in some turmoil. By 1925, he was listed by his diocese as 'on leave': he was clearly agonising over his future, as in December 1926 he and Edith were married at Penistone in Yorkshire, and he took the unusual step of becoming a Church of England clergyman.[118]

Catholic Social Teaching and 'after the war'

Chaplains found themselves responsible for helping the soldiers to fill idle hours between action, particularly towards the end of the war and immediately after, as they waited for demobilisation. They used some of that time to organise educational events, to help the men to envisage the possibilities of a different future. They would give talks to groups of soldiers, not just Catholics, sometimes on specifically religious subjects, such as a series on John Henry Newman,[119] but also on topics of common interest. Among the most popular of these was Catholic Social Teaching and thoughts of rebuilding society after the war led a number of chaplains to ask Parkinson for copies of his book, *A Primer of Social Science*, published in 1913 and often reprinted.[120]

This was the product of Parkinson's long and active engagement with Catholic Social Teaching and was quoted with approval by his longtime ally, Fr Charles Plater SJ, in his *Primer of Peace and War* (1915). Plater commended Parkinson as one of the few priests who had actually written about Catholic Social Teaching[121] and suggested that his *Primer* should be required reading for every priest.[122] In *The Priest and Social Action* Plater surveyed in some detail the work done in European and English seminaries to introduce the theology of Catholic Social Teaching, without undermining the existing curriculum of Philosophy and Theology. He stressed, on the basis of his knowledge of what Parkinson was doing at Oscott, that lectures on social issues must have 'a structured place in the philosophical and theological curriculum'.[123] He also commended the usefulness of informal seminars and study groups among seminarians, linked to the Catholic Social Guild, as Parkinson encouraged at Oscott.

Parkinson was one of a group of priests and lay people who had established the Catholic Social Guild (CSG) in 1909 to spread the teaching articulated by Pope Leo XIII in his encyclical *Rerum Novarum* of 1891. It was also a response to growing fears among the bishops and other Church leaders of the growing influence of Marxist Communism and its attendant dangers. Parkinson's stature as the longstanding Rector of Oscott was vital to the early CSG, and he had done much to encourage interest in social questions in the seminary long before the CSG was conceived. Priests who had passed through Oscott were deeply imbued with an appreciation of the social issues of the day and the Catholic response to them. Fr Joseph Lomax, a student at Oscott between 1904 and 1907, was among those who became involved in the early CSG, establishing a Catholic School for Social Science in Manchester, with Bishop Casartelli's blessing.[124] He later saw active service as a chaplain between 1915 and 1917, when he was invalided out, having been blown up and buried for a time in a shell hole. He died in 1941, aged 61, as parish priest of St Mary's, Levenshulme.[125]

Demobilisation and Disillusion

Parkinson himself was actively engaged in speaking to Catholic and non-Catholic groups on Catholic Social Teaching. The priests in his circle of acquaintance could not fail to be marked by his commitment to social issues, which would become so vital in the post war years. As one chaplain wrote to Parkinson: 'It is a subject which appeals to the men very much and it is a subject which has this in common with the other subjects treated, viz. that many men are surprised that there is a reasoned theory put forward by any Church about the matter.'[126] In the months following the Armistice, Fr Charles McDonnell found himself posted to Italy with the British troops who formed part of the Italian Expeditionary Force, and was giving talks to the men, based on Parkinson's book, on subjects including the role of the state, labour rights and the just wage. He also hoped to join a small pilgrimage of soldiers to Rome.[127] At the same time, Parkinson was increasingly involved in pressing for reform of the Poor Law and for unemployment insurance.[128]

The soldiers' openness to an alternative vision of society perhaps reflects the more general mood expressed in Lt. Col. Rowland Feilding's reflections, as he and his men waited for demobilisation in February 1919:

> The raging desire still continues to be demobilised quickly. Nevertheless, I feel pretty sure that, for many, there will be pathetic disillusionment. In the trenches the troops have had plenty of time for thought, and, as

'Happy Days'[the nickname of Fr Benedict Williamson, one of the best known chaplains] said the other day, there has grown up in their minds, a heavenly picture of England which does not exist, and never did exist, and never will exist as long as men are human.

After all, there was a good deal to be said in favour of the old trench life. There were none of the mean, haunting fears of poverty there, and the next meal – if you were alive to take it – was as certain as the rising sun. The rations were the same for the 'haves' and the 'have-nots', and the shells fell, without favour, upon both.

In a life where no money passes, the ownership of money counts for nothing. Rich and poor alike stand solely upon their individual merits, without discrimination. You can have no idea, till you have tried it, how much pleasanter life is under such circumstances. In spite of – or partly perhaps because of the gloominess of the surroundings – there was an atmosphere of selflessness and a spirit of camaraderie the like of which has probably not been seen in the world before, at least on so grand a scale.[129]

Cardinal Bourne, similarly aware that demobilisation would be unlikely to bring about the longed-for 'land fit for heroes' used the services of Charles Plater to draft his Pastoral Letter, *The Nation's Crisis*, in early 1918, which was widely circulated. It was deeply imbued with Catholic Social Teaching and hope for the possibilities of Catholic evangelisation in the post-war world.[130] In it, Bourne reflected upon the changed world that the war would produce: 'During the war the minds of people have been profoundly altered. Dull acquiescence in social injustice has given way to active discontent. The very foundations of our economic system, of morals and religion, are being sharply scrutinised...The army, for instance is not only fighting, it is also thinking...And the general effect of this on the young men who are the citizens of "after the War" is little short of revolutionary'.[131] Bourne continued to publish more in the same vein after the war, and actively to promote the work of the Catholic Social Guild, under Parkinson's leadership.

Armistice Day

Oscott, like the rest of the nation, waited agonisingly for the Armistice to be declared in November 1918. The anticipation of the German acceptance of the Allies' terms and the official proclamation of the cessation of hostilities grew to fever pitch as 11 November dawned. 'At 10.40 the first maroons were heard, followed at once by the noise of factory buzzers etc. The Vice Rector began at once to ring the tower bell, classes broke up and all work stopped for the day. At the end of dinner the Rector made a very short but appropriate speech, the national anthem was sung lustily and the Allies' success heartily drunk. In the afternoon all students were allowed to go into Birmingham to see the celebrations.[132]

Yet the reality was that the Armistice was generally greeted with numbness and relief rather than jubilation and celebration of victory. In a letter to chaplains, commending their work, Mgr William Keatinge and Fr Stephen Rawlinson acknowledged that, for the military chaplain, the cessation of hostilities 'must indeed be...a most happy relief'.[133] Whilst Catholics joined in the national thanksgiving for peace and victory, there were sober voices questioning the long-term impact of the loss and devastation on post-war society.

Post-War Reforms at Oscott

The chaplains also began to think of the future of the priesthood in England, and how the experience of war would affect the seminaries, particularly Oscott. They came across young men who had broken off from seminary to fight, and others who had expressed interest in a priestly vocation if they survived but all must have shared the reflection of Fr Ayles-Waters: 'tis a shame that their lives have been scarred with this terrible affair'.[134]

Fr Osmund Woods, a former Vice-Rector of Oscott was somewhat more optimistic: 'I would not be surprised if Oscott became filled again with students after the war, but especially with students following a short course. Life at the Front has made many of our young men think and pray, and I feel sure that a good number will find that they have a vocation for the priesthood. So far [early 1916] I have only had dealings with one such case, but when the bustle and interest of war is over many others will perhaps turn their thoughts to the priesthood'.[135] By the time the war was over, he was forecasting a golden future for Oscott: 'Oscott is on my mind as it always has been. I hope to see it take the leading

Fr Osmund Woods was Vice-Rector at Oscott (Birmingham Archdiocesan Archives)

position among the English seminaries. In certain points it has always done so; possibly now that peace is here it may flourish and become the training ground for as many students as its accommodation permits'.[136] Fr Woods' optimism was fulfilled. As men returned from the war, all the seminaries filled up again and by 1921, Oscott had 80 students. Among them were several former Anglican clergy received into the Church during the war, for whom 'seminary life must have been extremely burdensome', but who emerged to play an active part in the life of local parishes.[137]

In other respects, all was not well. The College Diary recorded that, in October 1918, there were recurrent indications of 'an unsatisfactory spirit' among the students. No detail is given, but aware that the end of the war would present its own issues the difficult atmosphere was taken seriously enough by the Rector to involve the Archbishop. He requested the Archbishop to set up a commission to look into aspects of life at Oscott. The result was a report laid before the College staff in January 1919 by Archbishop Ilsley, apparently 'much disturbed by it and greatly moved in reading it'. The reforms introduced at once seemed designed to bring about a more adult atmosphere in which the students were expected to exercise greater responsibility for themselves. Smoking was allowed in the grounds, the summer house and the billiard room, students were allowed to go out in twos and the timetable was altered to give greater freedom in the evening study hours.[138]

This was not the end of difficulties, as the College filled up with students bearing the scars and the greater maturity of the post-war generation. By 1922 a further commission, set up by Ilsley's successor, Archbishop John McIntyre, introduced reforms clearly intended to restore an atmosphere of piety, self-denial and seriousness of purpose to seminary life.[139] Parkinson was by then 70 and had been Rector for twenty five years and was perhaps losing his grip on a generation whose life experience he had only shared at second hand through the letters that had flowed into Oscott from military chaplains and serving men.

The programme of reforms was slow in taking effect. Philip Rhodes, the young man unable to leave his teaching post to enter the seminary, for fear of conscription, was only able to be ordained after the war in 1921. He was then sent to Fribourg where he took a doctorate, returning to teach theology and be Prefect of Studies at Oscott. Rhodes clearly expected high intellectual standards of himself and the seminarians. In one of his annual reports as Prefect of Studies, in 1927, he commented happily that the College now had a greater number of brilliant students and fewer who were 'thoroughly weak', but his complaint was of those who 'on account of the lack of energetic effort, remained in a position of mediocrity'.[140] Rhodes was appointed to the parish of Evesham in 1930, where he enhanced his scholarly reputation, not only as a theologian, but as an eminent botanist, with a particular interest in lichens and mosses and his collections of tens of thousands of specimens were donated to the Museum of Natural History, Kew Gardens and Birmingham Museum.[141]

An Expanding Church

For the Catholic Church in Britain, the immediate post-war years saw growing membership and increased attendance at Mass and the sacraments. Perhaps this was because Catholic theology and practice, both at home and in the battlefields, had confronted evil with a coherent, but not simplistic, response and because the Church offered a space where, not only remembrance, but prayer for the dead and an active consciousness of them were deliberately encouraged.

There was a sense of hopefulness among the English Catholics, especially the leadership, who were encouraged by high profile conversions such as G. K. Chesterton and Ronald Knox.

The powerful relationships forged between the serving soldiers and the chaplains amidst the horrors of war played no small part in the continuity of Catholic faith among the post war generation of men. In Birmingham this was demonstrated by the institution, in 1919, of the 'Men's Mass' on Easter Monday, which continues to the present day, but originated as an act of remembrance for those lost in the war.[142] The sentiments of one demobbed sergeant a decade after the war ended, may be typical: 'I am always open to testify to the wonderful devotion and fatherly spirit of our chaplains at the Mass, in camp, in the club, and finally on demob and civilian life, that wonderful golden link of friendship still lives on and will, please God, until we all enter the joy of the Lord'.[143]

Mgr Henry Parkinson died quite suddenly after a short illness in 1924. By then the world he had known had passed away, but the world and the Church stood much in need of the teaching on social justice that he had done so much to advocate. He was succeeded by Charles Cronin who had spent 16 years as Vice-Rector and acting Rector in the English College, Rome until he joined the Oscott staff, succeeding Joseph Whitfield as Vice-Rector in 1914. His time as Rector was happier and more fruitful than working under Parkinson as Vice-Rector, and he began a process of liberalisation of the rules. 'Before long, this liberalisation was to lead to a slackness in discipline...There did not seem to be any firm principles to take the place of the now abandoned arbitrary regime of Parkinson.'[144] Williams quotes one of the then students James Crichton on the effects on seminary life of the mix of 'ex-army men and "late vocations", who found the regime strenuous and trying. They were men, often in indifferent health, and those of us who had come straight from school were, well, schoolboys'.[145]

Mgr James Dey

In 1929, a Rector was appointed who was more than capable of empathising with the post-war generation and understood the effects of war on individual men and their approach to life. James Dey was a rarity among the Catholic chaplains of the First World War, in that he was not only a wartime chaplain, but gave most of his priestly life to military chaplaincy. Born in Walsall on 14 October 1869, Dey was one of the first to enter Oscott as a seminarian after the closure of the school in 1889. Ordained on 17 February 1894, he served on the staff of Cotton College until 1900 when he went for two years to St Edmund's College, Ware. Returning to Cotton

Fr James Dey as a young priest (Catholic Bishopric of the Forces)

in 1902, he was one of a number of staff who resigned over clashes of policy and personality.

In 1903 he became an army chaplain, serving in South and East Africa, beginning a career of nearly thirty years as chaplain to the forces. As one of the few regular army chaplains in 1914, he went to France at once with the British Expeditionary Force and went through the bloody retreat from Mons with the Connaught Rangers.

Dey was Mentioned in Despatches early in the war, in February 1915 after Ypres. His vivid and unsparing account of life at the Front was published by the newspaper in his home town of Walsall, where he was celebrated as a local hero.

At present we are in an empty house. We have managed to rake up a table and some chairs; for the rest, one does what one can with boxes and some empty bottles. There is a terrible din going on. The French are making a strong attack right in front of us, and there are several batteries going for all they are worth. You have no idea what a row three or four guns can kick up. This morning I said Mass in the village church. The church is about a mile away, down a side road, bordered with poplars, that leads straight down to the trenches and the German position. A little along it are the guns that boom out during Mass – great, deep-throated fellows. All the body of the church is filled with wounded French, lying on straw…Twice during my Mass this morning, stretcher bearers brought a dead soldier through the crowded sanctuary and set the body down on the floor where there were four others.

He goes on to recount how he helped a young Second Lieutenant to operate on a badly wounded Scots Guard by candlelight and torchlight, and how, afterwards, on a bitterly cold night, the two men had settled down in the warmest place they could find shelter – a large smouldering manure heap. Early next morning:

The rest of our ambulance came up. I found they had picked up a lot of wounded Germans, so I went round to see if there were any Catholics. The first waggon had four badly hit, three were Catholics and one a priest. Another chap had it in the stomach. I thought he would not last long, so I gave him the last sacraments, and an hour later I buried him.

He then came across a gun emplacement where the two German gunners had been killed by British field guns. The remains of their makeshift meal were left scattered around, and one of the dead soldiers was still clutching the letter from his sweetheart that he had been reading. Dey did not spare the grisly realities of war, describing how he had searched the shattered bodies for their identity discs, but before moving on, had slaked his own hunger by snatching up one of the meat chops still clenched in a dead man's hand.[146]

In 1916 James Dey was appointed senior Catholic Chaplain to the East Africa Force and, whilst there, was awarded the DSO. At the end of that campaign he returned to England as Bishop Keatinge's Vicar General, and at the end of the war was appointed Senior Catholic Chaplain to the newly formed Royal Air Force.

Probably due to his longstanding friendship with Archbishop Thomas Williams, also a military chaplain, he was asked to be Rector of Oscott in 1929. Williams was born locally and studied at Oscott from 1893 to 1900. He read history at Cambridge after ordination, and taught briefly at Cotton College, but was caught in the same disputes that led to Dey's departure in 1902-3. Education continued to be his life, however, and he spent three years on the staff of St Edmund's Ware, before becoming a highly successful master of St Edmund's House, Cambridge.

A group of Oscotians taken after the war. Standing: J. Collins, Brian Withers, John Drinkwater, M. Byrne; Seated: George Craven, W. Withers, Francis Drinkwater (courtesy of Dr Marie Rowlands).

In October 1916 Dey built a much-needed chapel at St Edmund's, but 'once the chapel had been completed, the Master's interests began to drift away from St Edmund's and turn towards the war'.[147] The number of resident priests at St Edmund's dropped, while the overdraft grew, but the governing body insisted on staying open, while Williams increasingly felt that Cambridge was 'no place for a man who was physically fit enough to get into uniform'.[148] He was able to find an outlet for his frustration as chaplain to two military hospitals at Cherry Hinton and Barnwell, and later at the First Eastern General Hospital. In May 1917, he pleaded unsuccessfully to be allowed to step down as Master, but eventually, in January

1918, his own bishop, Ilsley of Birmingham agreed to his giving 12 months' notice of resignation, in order to join the army as a forces chaplain. He wrote back to Ilsley: 'It is work which appeals to me more than anything I have done, and I should very much like to see the war through and keep on working as a chaplain until it is over. In fact, it is very difficult to feel any interest in anything else while there is such war work to be done'.[149]

In May 1918 his resignation was accepted and Fr Joseph Whitfield was appointed to succeed him. A month later, Williams was accepted for military chaplaincy service in France. By then the war was in its last months, and most of his service was with the British Army of the Rhine, the occupying force based in Cologne after hostilities ended. Following demobilisation in 1920, he picked up the threads of higher education, as head of St Charles' House, Oxford, a house of studies for diocesan priests. Two years later, he succeeded Edward Hymers, the man with whom he had so bitterly disagreed, as headmaster of Cotton College.[150]

Dey had just retired from his post with the RAF as Williams was appointed to be Archbishop of Birmingham, so it may have seemed a perfect arrangement to the new archbishop; the years Dey spent at Oscott were his only ones away from military life. The indications are that his leadership of the seminary was, not surprisingly, strongly shaped by his military background. Mgr Francis Davis, one of his colleagues at Oscott, recalled that, 'Mgr Dey was for introducing the way of mutual trust and free discipline which exists among a group of officers. He thought that the students should be regarded as officers in God's army and that they were mature enough, sincere enough and sufficiently educated to act as gentlemen, if they were treated as such.'[151]

After seven years as Rector of Oscott, he succeeded Keatinge and was named Bishop of Sebastopolis and Bishop of the Forces on 2 June 1935, meaning that he led the Catholic chaplaincy to the British armed forces throughout the Second World War. He died of cancer only a year after the war ended, in the summer of 1946. The *Birmingham Post* obituary described Dey as: 'An excellent speaker, one of the leading thinkers of the Catholic hierarchy and in every way a virile "man's man" with a fund of deep Christian charity that made him welcome everywhere'.[152]

Dey retained his affection for Cotton College, although his early career there was blighted by changes in personnel and policy without which he would have

Archbishop Thomas Williams, Bishop James Dey, Cardinal Arthur Hinsley and Bishop James Moriarty of Shrewsbury at Bishop James Dey's consecration as Bishop of the Forces at Oscott on 3 June 1935. (Birmingham Archdiocesan Archives)

probably fulfilled what he felt to be a calling to be a priest-schoolmaster. The content of his will suggests that his heart was much closer to Cotton than to Oscott. Apart from family bequests, his executors, Fr Joseph Dunn, headmaster of Cotton, and Canon Francis de Capitain, parish priest in Sutton Coldfield, were directed to leave his books to Cotton, and to use the residue of his estate to establish scholarships for Church students at Cotton. The only mention of Oscott was the personal bequest of a gold chalice to his old colleague on the staff, Mgr Francis Davis.[153] Even the Archbishop of Westminster commented on this but tactfully assumed that Dey 'felt that the needs of Cotton to be greater than those of Oscott'.[154]

Yet Dey did choose to be ordained bishop at Oscott, and to be buried in the shadow of the chapel in which his ordination took place in 1935. His time at Oscott was evidently a fruitful but challenging one. A Scottish priest from the Archdiocese of Edinburgh who was at Oscott under Dey recollected over fifty years later his relief that he had been there in Dey's time because, before then, there were seemingly endless rules. Dey announced on his arrival that: 'There are no Rules of this House – but some wishes of the community'. He recalled with gratitude Dey's encouragement of his students, including himself, nurturing speaking and acting skills to improve public speaking and preaching and how the Rector had improved his capacity for early rising by giving him the job of ringing the bell to wake the rest of the house.[155] Dey's vision for the running of Oscott was to treat the students as he would fellow officers, expecting a high degree of mutual trust and responsibility but his obituarist had to admit that this was somewhat idealistic and that most students were not ready for that level of responsibility.[156]

Another of his great friends, fellow Birmingham priest and First World War chaplain, was Fr Samuel Gosling who sent notes to 'Cap' (Canon De Capitain) for obituaries. In recounting the bare facts of Dey's life, he asserted that it was impossible to 'convey a true picture of the strong and forceful personality to whom these things happened':

> Few men would have had the courage to initiate the changes he made, and perhaps no one but Dey himself could have carried them to the success that he could rightly claim for these departures from tradition. The secret lay, where the secret of achievement so often does lie, in that indefinable but recognisable quality that we call personality, and James Dey's personality was the most recognisable thing about him. It was compact [sic] of honesty of purpose integrity of principle and fearlessness of utterance, and it was as evident in his outward appearance and manner as in his spirit – in his straightforward glance, in his firm handshake and in the incisiveness of his speech and the directness of his talk, never free for long from that subacid [sic] tone he affected that so delighted his friends because although it sometimes stung it never left a scar.[157]

Samuel Gosling was one of a generation of post-war priests much influenced by Dey, Thomas Williams and William Barry and a man of wide literary, sporting and cultural interests. Like his contemporary Francis Drinkwater, he became absorbed in the cause of Catholic education and for nine years in the 1930s he edited the journal founded by Drinkwater to advance children's catechesis, *The Sower*, before returning for a second period as a wartime army chaplain in World War II. Friends questioned his decision to rejoin and it may have weakened his health, but 'the army had a peculiar attraction for him, partly perhaps because it represented so much of what is English; it certainly appealed to his marked patriotism, his love of precision and his genius for organisation'.[158] In other respects, Gosling was a man of a new era, founding a society and a magazine to advance the cause of English in the liturgy and gained a wide reputation as a writer on the subject. He did not live to see an English liturgy, dying in 1950. 'Always a strong, firmly decided character, he had nevertheless a perfect genius for friendship; his wit was keen, his humour entertaining and his manner was full of delightful charm.'[159]

The Catholic Land Association

The seminary was not the only sphere in which Dey was an idealist. He had, like all Oscotians of his generation, been imbued by Parkinson with the principles of Catholic Social Teaching and these principles became a serious element in Catholic involvement in the rebuilding of British society after 1918. The 1920s and 1930s were times of severe economic and social stress and among the possible solutions offered was the movement known as Distributism, which owed much to Catholic Social Teaching. It took its principles from *Rerum Novarum* and from the reiteration of Catholic Social Teaching, *Quadragesimo Anno*, issued by Pius XI in 1931, advocating an economic system based on the widest possible distribution of ownership of the means of production. This was promoted as an alternative both to large scale capitalism and ownership by the few and to communism and control of production by the state. Distributism drew much Catholic support and among its English promoters were G. K. Chesterton and Hilaire Belloc.

An offshoot of Distributism was the Catholic Land Association, another response to the overwhelming industrialisation and urbanisation of England in the drive for manufacturing success. It echoed some of the vision of earlier romantic radicals, including William Morris, John Ruskin and the Arts and Crafts Movement but had a specifically Catholic dimension, drawn from Catholic Social Teaching. It began in Scotland in 1929 and came to an end at the outbreak of the Second World War.

College gardener, Henry Bullivent tending the onion crop in the post-war years. (The Bullivent family)

James Dey became closely involved in the Catholic Land Association during his time at Oscott, as the founding president of the Midland branch of the Association on 31 March 1931. It recruited over 350 members, with some support from Archbishop Williams but the national association did not attract episcopal or governmental support. Williams was an active advocate of Catholic Social Teaching and President of the Catholic Social Guild from 1937; he encouraged the revival of the Catholic Social Guild in Oscott, where it rose quickly from around a dozen members to fifty.[160]

Dey took up the challenge of articulating a Catholic response to the social ills of contemporary society, about which Parkinson had been so concerned and of which the wartime chaplains had become so aware. The specific aim of the Catholic Land Association was to bring Catholics to appreciate the need to recreate Catholic rural life in Britain and to encourage Catholic factory workers to repopulate the countryside and nurture a renewal of simplicity of existence and a Catholic way of life. James Dey worked closely with a local Sutton man, Harold

Robbins, himself a veteran of the First World War and a convert to Catholicism. Despite advancing disability, Robbins was 'one of the most devoted and strenuous leaders' of the Catholic Land Movement. Robbins acted as secretary of the Midland branch of the Land Association and his home, Weeford Cottage, on the edge of Sutton Coldfield, became 'a place of pilgrimage for priests'.

> He set to work to get into touch with all people of similar views and to collect them together into a Catholic Land Association. The ideal he set before it was to establish a truly Catholic village in each diocese, with the Mass as centre of its life and every activity of agriculture and craftsmanship organized around it as an act of worship. Not one of his critics—Catholic or non-Catholic—realized better than he himself what a terrific task, what a heroic enterprise he was setting his hand to. He was sacrificing his life for what could not possibly bring him or anyone else fame or profit. All that concerned him was to set up a shining example of Catholic social justice in actual being for all men to see.[161]

A rare publication by Dey was an essay in Hilaire Belloc's *Flee to the Fields*, effectively the manifesto of the Catholic Land Movement, published in 1934. Dey discussed the 'religious advantages' of Catholics, whom he believed to be in real moral danger, leaving the industrial towns for the countryside. By leaving the towns Catholics might escape the pernicious influence of the spread of Communism. Catholics, being heavily represented among the poorer, urban parts of the population were being more harshly hit by the industrial depression, and were, he believed, more vulnerable to ideological extremists. If Catholics moved to the countryside in numbers, it would spread the faith more widely and bringing Catholics into closer contact with the natural world would restore a simplicity of faith and tackle the problem of 'leakage' or loss of Catholics. Life in the country, he concluded, 'when judged by religious and moral standards, being safer and saner in itself than life in a town, ought to be made possible for more Catholics than those who follow it at the present time'.[162]

A letter of support from the Secretary of State to the Holy See, Cardinal Pacelli, later Pius XII, was received in 1933, but the bishops of England and Wales offered no such support. The Land Movement was dealt its death blow when the bishops refused to sanction an annual national collection to fund its activities. 'Robbins commented bitterly that "the Catholic authorities in England have never shown any other sentiment than embarrassment to have their principles stated so eloquently".'[163]

Flee to the Fields?

The title chosen by Belloc for his collection of essays, *Flee to the Fields*, carries a possibly unconscious, echo of John McCrae's famous 1915 poem, beginning 'In Flanders' fields, the poppies blow...' The experience of Flanders' fields had shaped the generation of those who had survived its horrors; they wanted the blood shed there to be a fruitful sacrifice. For English Catholics, the experience of the war had 'set patriotism within its appropriate framework, and, in so doing, purified it'.[164] It had also nurtured, as well as militarism and violent bloodshed, certain values that the survivors would take home with them.

Lt Col Rowland Feilding had reflected, perhaps shockingly, that, in terms of the basic Christian values, there were worse ways of life than that of the trenches, where 'there was an atmosphere of selflessness and a spirit of camaraderie the like of which has probably not been seen in the world before, at least on so grand a scale'.[165] The war gave urgency to the desire to embed the teaching of the Gospel in the way in which society organised itself, set out by Leo XIII and articulated for English Catholics by Henry Parkinson, Charles Plater, Cardinal Francis Bourne and the chaplains who sought to educate the serving men in the ideals of Catholic Social Teaching. In the next generation, those ideals were taken up by James Dey, Fr Vincent McNabb OP, G. K. Chesterton and Hilaire Belloc and the Distributists. The Catholic Land Movement was one of the romantic, idealistic, perhaps naive expressions of a profoundly Catholic desire for a renewed society and a different, and fundamentally Catholic, way of life, which, by the 1930s, was doomed to be destroyed all over again by the machinery of war.

Appendix 1

Oscotians commemorated on the Oscott College war memorial

- **Major Jasper Howley** DSO; Oscott 1881-85; the first recorded Oscotian to die in the war.

  Died 11 March 1915 aged 46. Commanding 2nd Battalion Lincolnshire Regiment.

  Grave III. A. 3 Rue Petillon Military Cemetery, Fleurbaix, Pas de Calais, France.

- **Lieutenant Colonel William Francis Dugmore** MinD, DSO; Oscott 1881-6

  Died 12 June 1917 aged 48. North Staffs Regiment.

  Grave VII.N.1 Railway Dugouts Burial Ground (Transport Farm) West Vlaanderen, Belgium.

- **Lieutenant Colonel Thomas Xavier Britten** MinD; Oscott 1882-6

  Died 15 April 1915 aged 46. 110th Mahratta Light Infantry.

  Grave III. G. 1 Basra War Cemetery, Iraq

- **Lieutenant Colonel Victor Mottet de la Fontaine** MinD, DSO; Oscott 1871-75, 1886 - 89

  Died 5 August 1917 aged 44. East Surrey Regiment 9th Battalion.

  Grave III.C. 15 Reninghelst New Military Cemetery, West Vlaanderen, Belgium.

- **Father Herbert Henry John Collins** Oscott 1902-8

  Died 9 April 1917 aged 35. Chaplain Black Watch.

  Grave XVII.K.10 Caberet-Rouge British Cemetery, Souchez, Pas de Calais, France.

- **2nd Lieutenant Joseph Arnold;** Oscott 1903-5

  Died 2 September 1918. Manchester Regiment 18th Battalion Attached 1/5th Battalion

  Grave B8 Manchester Cemetery Riencourt-les-Bapaume, Pas de Calais, France

- **Bombadier John Molloy;** Oscott 1906-10

  Died 21 March 1918 aged 29. Royal Garrison Artillery 113th Heavy Battery.

  No known grave. Commemorated Bay 1, Arras Memorial, Pay de Calais, France.

- **Private Leo Thomas Bernard Kelly;** Oscott 1908 –1909

  Died 1 April 1918. 20th Hussars.

  No known grave. Commemorated Panel 6 Pozieres Memorial, Somme, France.

- **Lieutenant William Ignatius George Farren;** Oscott 1914

  Died 29 March 1918 aged 25. Old Ground 7, St Peblig Churchyard, Caernarvon.

- **Sergeant Bartholomew Scanlon;** Oscott 1914-15

  Died 31 January 1916 aged 21. Cameron Highlanders 5th Batt. Grave C 15 Hyde Park Corner (Royal Berks) Cemetery, Hainault, Belgium.

- **Flight Lieutenant Oscar Drinkwater;** Oscott 1914-1916

  Died 23 August 1918 aged 23. Grave VIII. H.10 Brown's Road Military Cemetery, Festubert, Pas de Calais.

- **2nd Lieutenant Joseph Bernaerts (Belgian Army);** Oscott 1914 –1915

  Died 5 November 1918 aged 24. Oudenaard Cemetery, Belgium

- **Lance Corporal John Stokes;** Oscott 1916

  Died on 8 October 1918 aged 24. Grave III.B.10, Prospect Hill Cemetery, Gouy, Aisne.

Appendix 2

Oscotian Military Chaplains (RAChD – Royal Army Chaplains' Department)

Rev. Walter Amery, Westminster, born 27 March 1879; Oscott 11 September 1901 – 15 August 1905; RAChD 4th class 14 May 1915, France and Egypt, 11 May 1922

Rev. George Ayles-Waters, Salford, born 16 April 1885; Oscott 2 September 1914 – 3 March 1917; RAChD 4th class 1914 – 17, France and Mespotamia 15 January 1918 – 29 January 1922, died 1945

Rev. George Ignatius Boniface, Southwark, born 31 July 1874; Oscott 6 November 1894 – 31 March 1900; RAChD 4th class Egypt 1 April 1915 – 2 September 1916 (ill health); died 7 February 1940

Rev. John O'Riordan Browne M C (Bar), Salford, born 3 August 1892, Oscott 14 September 1914 – 2 May 1916; RAChD 4th class 1914 – 16, France 31July 1917 – 6 April 1919

Rev. William George Bunce, Birmingham, born 10 February 1888; Oscott 5 September 1906 – 8 December 1912; RAChD 4th class France 23 October 1918 – 18 July 1920; died 1937

Rev. George Boniface (Birmingham Archdiocesan Archives)

Rev. George Carlisle, Westminster, born 3 July 1885, Oscott 10 September 1902 – 12 July 1908 RAChD 4th class 25 May 1915 Belgium, France, Egypt, Palestine, Germany. Remained in army chaplaincy after war, awarded OBE; 1931 became a Chaplain, 3rd Class (with rank of Major). Retired 1932 and no longer listed in *Catholic Directory*.

Rev. Herbert Henry Collins, Westminster, born 27 December 1881; Oscott 10 September 1902 – 12 July 1908; RAChD 3 June 1915, killed France 9 April 1917

Rev. Major George Laurence Craven M C, Birmingham, born 1 February 1884, Oscott 10 September 1902 – 29 June 1912; RAChD 3rd class 25 May 1916 – 24 April 1919 France (later Auxiliary Bishop in Westminster)

Rt Rev. Mgr. James Dey DSO V C, Birmingham, born 14 October 1869; Oscott 16 September 1889 – 17 February 1894; RAChD 7 August 1903 – 9 December 1918 Egypt, France, E Africa; relinquished commission on appointment as Principal Chaplain RAF (later Bishop of the Forces)

Rev. William Crawford Donleavy, Westminster, born 10 June 1872; Oscott 18 March 1893 – 21 September 1895; RAChD 4th class 4 March 1915 France – 19 August 1919

Rev. William Dorran, Salford, born 2 October 1888; Oscott 13 October 1914 – 18 July 1915; RAChD 4th class 30 October 1917 – 21 February 1920 France; died 25 May 1955

Rev. Major Francis Harold Drinkwater, Birmingham, born 3 August 1886, Oscott 9 September 1903 – 16 October 1910; RAChD 3rd class 18 May 1915 – 24 May 1919 France; died 1982

Rev. Joseph Dwyer, Birmingham, born 7 January 1889; Oscott 11 September 1907 – 15 August 1913; RAChD 4th class 10 January 1916 – 0 May 1919 Salonika

Rev. Wilfred Foley, Westminster, born 19 June 1871: Oscott 1893 – 94; RAChD 1915, Egypt, Serbia; died 21 November 1922

Rev. Samuel Joseph Gosling, Birmingham, born 18 April 1883; Oscott 10 September 1902 – 10 September 1908; RAChD 4th class 25 May 1915 – 3 July 1919 France and Italy; died 1950

Rev. Eric Francis Green, Westminster, born 13 January 1870; Oscott 18 March 1893 – 29 February 1896; Royal Naval Division Chaplain 4th class 1914 – 1917 France and Gallipoli

Rev. Ernest Jarvis, Birmingham, born 25 August 1875; Oscott 20 January 1894 – 4 May 1901; RAChD 4th class 18 December 1917 – 10 June 1919 France, Attached to RAMC, awarded MC October 1918

Rev. Francis Lockett, Birmingham, born 29 October 1889; Oscott 11 September 1907 – 7 March 1914; RAChD 4th class 1 May 1917 – 11 March 1919 France

Rev. Joseph Edmund Lomax, Salford, born 12 April 1880; Oscott 7 September 1904 – 2 December 1907; RAChD 1915 – 17 (invalided out); died 2 February 1940

Rev. Charles G. McDonnell, Birmingham, born 10 May 1884; Oscott 7 September 1904 – 1 March 1911; RAChD 4th class 15 March 1916 – 9 November 1919 France, Egypt, Salonika

Rev. Francis Thomas McMahon, Portsmouth, born 18 February 1890; Oscott 26 March 1914 – 4 October 1915; RAChD 4th class 2 February 1917 – 21 October 1919 France

Rev. Edward Mostyn, Southwark, born 25 July 1870; Oscott 30 September 1889 – 21 December 1895; Naval Chaplain, China Station 1902 – 1905; RAChD 4th class 31 December 1914 – 15 April 1920 France, Italy, Gallipoli; died 23 February 1936

Rev. Timothy J O'Connell, Clifton, born 1 August 1890; Oscott 12 September 1912 – 15 July 1914 (left before ordination); RAChD 4th class 13 April 1917 – 1 November 1919 Mesopotamia, Russia

Very Rev. Mgr. Charles William Smith DSO OBE, Birmingham (later Plymouth and Northampton), born 3 February 1873; Oscott 17 January 1909 – 26 June 1909; RAChD 24 April 1915 France, Belgium, Mesopotamia; Assistant Principal Chaplain 1st class 1917, retired as Principal Catholic Chaplain 1930, died 1954

Rev. Randolph Richard Traill, Birmingham, born 6 September 1863; Oscott 19 October 1908 – 26 November 1912; RAChD 4th class 13 October 1916 – 5 March 1918 France

Rev. Major Joseph Whitfield DSO, Westminster/ Brentwood, born 16 December 1876, Oscott 5 September 1900 – 24 September 1904; Vice-Rector 1910 – 14; RAChD 3rd class 29 August 1914 – 24 April 1918 France, died 1961

Rev. Thomas Cuthbert Leighton Williams, Birmingham, born 20 March 1877; Oscott 7 September 1893 – 24 August 1900; RAChD June 1918 –1920 (British Army of the Rhine). Archbishop of Birmingham 1935; died 1946

Rev. Osmund Woods, Vice-Rector 1902 – 4; RAChD 4th class 6 May 1915 – 6 May 1916 France

Appendix 3

Oscotians known to have served in the armed forces

Dates indicate time at Oscott

+ indicates died during the war

Stephen Barber 1909 – 10

Captain Hubert Berkeley 1884

Lieutenant Colonel T. Mowbray Berkeley nd

James Bligh, Royal Fleet Auxiliary 1914 – 17

Eustace Blundell 1879 – 82

Jerome Coleman, Royal Garrison Auxiliary 1917

Colonel Raymond Crawford 1870 – 71

Colonel Rudolph Fielding, Earl of Denbigh CVO 1871 – 75

Captain the Honourable Charles Dormer, Royal Navy, CBE., J P 1873 – 76

Brigadier General Archibald Campbell Douglas-Dick CB, CMG 1862

Brigadier General J H Elmsley DSO CMG, CB 1887 – 89

+Captain John Joseph Esmonde MP 1876 – 80

Colonel Edward Farrell 1874

+Captain John E Farrell JP DL 1873 – 78

The Honourable Everard Fielding 1877 – 79

Brigadier General Percy Desmond Fitzgerald DSO 1885 – 89 MinD, Croix d'Officier of the Legion of Honour

Rear Admiral the Honourable Edward Fitzherbert CB 1875 – 77

Captain the Honourable Thomas Fitzherbert (Albert Medal) 1879 – 86

Major the Honourable Hugh Fraser MVO

2nd Lieutenant Leslie Gardner, Royal Army Medical Corps 1914

2nd Lieutenant Christopher Gilshenan 1914

Brigadier General Sir H Grattan-Bellew, Bart. 1873 – 77

Brigadier General Laurence Grattan-Esmonde 1876 – 82

+2nd Lieutenant Geoffrey J. Grattan Esmonde 1885 – 86; Northumberland Fusiliers, 26th (Tyneside Irish) Battalion; died 7 October 1916; grave III. A. 18 Cité Bonjean Military Cemetery, Armentières

Leading Seaman Patrick Heffernan 1907 – 08

Major General Sir Ivor Herbert, Bart. CB, CM, MP 1863 – 69

Major General W B Hickie KCB 1876 – 83 MinD

Brigadier General Carlos J Hickie CMG 1884 – 88 MinD

Lieutenant Colonel Henry Howley 1886 – 89

Colonel W F Leese 1866 – 70

James Lewis, Royal Garrison Auxiliary 1915 – 17

Lieutenant Colonel Reginald Longueville 1879 – 83

Captain Thomas Wilson Lynch 1880 – 86

Richard McClymont 1883 – 84

James McKenna 1914

Felix D McSwiney nd

2nd Lieutenant Alfred McVickers 1911 – 12

Gerald Magrath 1887 – 89

William Mann 1914 – 18

Lieutenant Colonel Edward Mostyn 1869 – 73

+Colonel Hon Edward Noel (rtd) 1866 – 70

Laurence J Petre 1878 – 81

Lieutenant Colonel Cuthbert J Pike 1880 – 84

Lieutenant Colonel Gerard Prendergast 1876 – 78

Lieutenant Colonel Philip Radcliffe, Royal Engineers, CMG 1874 – 80

Henry Radcliffe 1874 – 80

Sub-Lieutenant. Leonard Ross, Royal Naval Volunteer Reserve 1916 – 17

Michael A Russell, Royal Naval Division 1915 – 17

Lieutenant John J. Ryan 1882 – 88

Major Thomas Shepard 1874 – 78

Lieutenant Colonel Reginald Slaughter MinD, DSO 1887 – 89

Probationer Surgeon Charles Slim, Royal Navy 1908 – 10

Major Robert Smyth 1881 – 84

2nd Lieutenant Bernard Stanton 1906 – 10

Lieutenant Edward J Stonor 1877 – 83

2nd Lieutenant Ernest Sumner 1888 – 89

Lieutenant George Sumner 1886 – 89

Lieutenant Reginald Talbot 1885 – 89

Major General Lord Treowen CB, CMG 1863 – 69

2nd Lieutenant James Weston 1908 – 10

Cyril Wilson 1862 – 68

In the Belgian Army

Honore d'Hollander 1915

Paul Goris 1914 – 15

Ferdinand van Trimpont 1915 – 16

Abbreviations

CB – Companion of the Order of the Bath

CMG – Order of St Michael and St George

DSO – Distinguished Service Order

CBE – Commander of the Order of the British Empire

CVO – Commander Royal Victorian Order

KCB – Knight Commander of the Order of the Bath

MinD – Mentioned in Despatches

MVO – Member of the Royal Victorian Order

Appendix 4

Oscotian family members among the war dead

Lieutenant George Archer-Shee son of late Lieutenant Colonel Sir Martin Archer-Shee, DSO, born May 5, 1873, the son of Martin Archer-Shee and his wife Elizabeth née Pell of New York; Conservative politician; Oscott April 1859 – Summer 1862

Captain Edward Bagshawe, son of Judge William Henry Bagshawe, Oscott 1838 – 43; Yorkshire Regiment; died 20 June 1916, aged 36; grave VII.D.12 La Laiterie Cemetery, West Vlaanderen, Belgium

Lieutenant Gerald T M Colegrave

Captain Maurice Dease VC son of Edmund F Dease, Oscott 1873 – 78 and Katherine M. Dease, of Levington, Mullingar, Co. Westmeath; Royal Fusiliers 4th Battalion; died 23 August 1914 aged 24; grave V.B.2 St. Synphorien Military Cemetery, Hainault, Belgium. One of the first British officer battle casualties of the war, and the first posthumous recipient of the VC of the war. Citation 16 November 1914: 'Though two or three times badly wounded he continued to control the fire of his machine guns at Mons on 23 August until all his men were shot. He died of his wounds.'

Midshipman John Henry Grattan Esmonde, son of Sir Thomas Henry Grattan Esmonde, Bart. MP of Ballynastragh, Gorey, Co. Wexford, Oscott 1874 – 79; Royal Navy *HMS Invincible*, died 31 May 1917 aged 17; Memorial Portsmouth Naval Memorial panel 7.

Lieutenant Commander the Honourable Hugh R, Fielding, son of the Hon. J D Fitzgerald, KC Oscott 1858 – 65; Durham Light Infantry 15th Battalion; died 30 December 1915; grave II. B. 34 Houplines Communal Cemetery Extension, Nord.

Captain Gerald T Fitzgerald

Captain Thomas Fitzherbert-Brockholes son of William Fitzherbert-Brockholes, Oscott 1863 – 68

2nd Lieutenant Arthur Philip Fletcher, son of Robert Henry Fletcher, Oscott 1856 – 57

Major William A Grattan-Bellew MC, son of Henry Grattan-Bellew, of Mount Bellew, Co. Galway, Oscott 1873 – 77 (also served in 1914 18 war); Royal Flying Corps 29th Squadron and Connaught Rangers; died 24 March 1917 aged 23; grave III. C. 3 Avesnes le Comte Communal Cemetery Extension, Pas de Calais, France.

Lieutenant Joseph J Maxwell-Stuart, son of Edmund Maxwell-Stuart of Linden, East Lulworth, Dorset, Oscott 1870 – 75; Duke of Wellington's (West Riding Regiment) 9th Battalion; died 2 March 1916 aged 19; grave I. D. 6 Reninghelst New Military Cemetery, West Vlaanderen, Belgium. The youngest, and first, of four brothers killed in the war.

Edmund Joseph Maxwell-Stuart, son of Edmund Maxwell Stuart; Royal Engineers 175th Company; died 26 April 1916 aged 23; grave I.B. 29 Poperinghe New Military Cemetery, West Vlaanderen, Belgium. The second of four brothers killed in the war.

2nd Lieutenant Henry Joseph Ignatius Maxwell-Stuart, son of Edmund Maxwell-Stuart; Coldstream Guards 3rd Battalion; died 9 October 1917 aged 30; grave VIII. E. 1 Artillery Wood Cemetery, West Vlaanderen, Belgium. The third of four brothers killed in the war.

Lieutenant Alfred Joseph Maxwell-Stuart, son of Edmund Maxwell Stuart; Coldstream Guards 1st Battalion; died 24 August 1918 aged 20; grave IV. D. 11 Bagneux British Cemetery, Gezaincourt, Somme, France. The fourth of four brothers killed in the war.

Captain Piers Mostyn

Captain Edward Murphy son of Jerome Murphy, Oscott 1846 – 49

Francois de Mussy son of Philippe de Mussy, Oscott 1866 – 71

Henri de Mussy son of Philippe de Mussy, Oscott 1866 – 71

Major Edward F D Nicholson

Captain The Hon. William Nugent

Captain Arthur Radcliffe

Major Clement Ryan

Captain James H A Ryan son of Walter H Ryan MD, Oscott 1866 – 71; The King's (Liverpool Regiment) 1st Battalion; died 29 September 1915; grave D 16 Cambrin Military Cemetery, Pas de Calais, France

2nd Lieutenant Bernard A Shepherd

2nd Lieutenant Francis Joseph Silvertop, son of Henry Thomas Silvertop, of Minster Acres, Northumberland, Oscott 1864 – 72; Queen's Own Oxfordshire Hussars; died 20 May 1917 aged 33; grave II. E. 41 Templeux le Guerard British Cemetery, Somme, France

2nd Lieutenant Charles George Augustine Sibeth, son of Charles Joseph Sibeth, Oscott 1859 – 65; Royal Engineers; died 9 August 1915; memorial Menin Gate, Ypres, Belgium

2nd Lieutenant Cuthbert A Stonor

The Hon. Howard Stonor son of 4th Baron Camoys, Oscott 1869 – 72; 4th Battalion, attached 2nd Battalion South Staffordshire Regiment; died 10 March 1915, aged 21; memorial panel 10 and 11,Le Touret, Pas de Calais, France

Lieutenant Reginald de Trafford son of Cuthbert Sigismunde de Trafford of Croston Hall, Preston, Oscott 1877 – 80; King's Own (Royal Lancaster Regiment) 3rd Battalion attached Gloucestershire Regiment; died 9 May 1915; grave II.D.10. Le Touret Military Cemetery, Richebourge-L'Avoue, Pas de Calais, France

Lieutenant Ralph de Trafford son of Galfrid de Trafford Oscott 1882 - 86; Royal Fusiliers; died 25 April 1915 aged 22; memorial panel 37-41, Helles Memorial, Gallipoli, Turkey

Lieutenant Henry B Welman, son of Henry Acton Welman, Oscott 1864 – 74; Royal Marine Light Infantry HMS Victory; died 13 November 1916 aged 23; grave I.b.28 Mailly Wood Cemetery, Mailly-Maillet, Somme, France

2nd Lieutenant William J. Wolseley, son of Edward Talbot Wolseley, Oscott 1860 – 64; 2nd Battalion East Lancashire Regiment; died 12 March 1915 aged 29; grave III.D.19 Royal Irish Rifles Graveyard, Laventie, Pas de Calais, France

Lieutenant Charles Woodward son of Colonel Charles C Woodward, Oscott 1864 – 67, served as a Papal Zouave at the Battle of Mentana.

Endnotes

1   Inscription on the grave of Fr Herbert Collins, the only Oscotian chaplain killed in action in the First World War (courtesy of: The War Graves Photographic Project)

2   Katherine Finlay, *British Catholic Identity during the First World War: the Challenge of Universality and Particularity*, Oxford D Phil. 2004, p 2

3   Mark Vickers, *By the Thames Divided: Cardinal Bourne in Southwark and Westminster*, Gracewing, Leominster, 2013, p 326

4   Birmingham Archdiocesan Archives (BAA) D3254, 7 August 1914

5   BAA, D3253 7 August 1914

6   Obituary, *The Oscotian Magazine*, Summer 1951, pp 54 - 55

7   BAA OCA2/7/A/3 Martin Archer-Shee to Henry Parkinson, 15 November 1912

8   William Purdy, *Roman Catholic Chaplains During the First World War: Roles, Experiences and Dilemmas*, University of Central Lancashire MA, 2012, p 13

9   Purdy, p 14

10 William Barry, *Memories and Opinions*, London, Putnam's, 1926, p 268

11 *Royal Leamington Spa Courier and Warwickshire Standard*, 11 June 1915

12 Sheridan Gilley, 'Barry, William Francis (1849–1930)', Oxford Dictionary of National Biography, Oxford University Press, Sept 2012
    [http://www.oxforddnb.com/view/article/42351, accessed 15 July 2015]

13 *The Coventry Standard*, 10 - 11 November 1917

14 BAA OCA/5/1/2/4 Correspondence relating to the Apostolic Union of Secular Clergy in England, filed by year. (BAA/OCA/AUP) 1915 file, John Rowan to Henry Parkinson, 1 November 1915

15 *Birmingham Evening Despatch*, 4 June 1915

16 BAA OCA2/9/16/5/A/12 Walter Amery to Henry Parkinson nd 1905

17 BAA/OCA/AUP 1917 file, G Browne to Henry Parkinson, 8 September 1917

18 BAA/OCA2/1/3 Oscott College Diary 1901-32

19 BAA/OCA/AUP 1915 file, Augustine Emery to Henry Parkinson, 26 October 1915

20 BAA/OCA/AUP 1916 file, Godric Kean to Henry Parkinson 4 November 1916

21 BAA/OCA2/9/16/5/B/41 Joseph Bernaerts to Henry Parkinson 8 September 1915

22 BAA/OCA/AUP 1916 file, Joseph Geraghty to Henry Parkinson, nd 1916

23 Obituary, *St Bede's College Magazine,* 1968

24 BAA/OCA/2/9/16/5/F/5 Isabel Farren to Henry Parkinson 24 July 1918

25 David Milburn, *A History of Ushaw College*, Ushaw, 1964, p 314

26 Finlay, p 125

27 BAA/OCA OS/2/7/F/3 Frederick Furniss to Henry Parkinson nd July 1918

28 BAA/OCA/AUP 1915 file, Joseph Chambers to Henry Parkinson 25 October 1915

29 BAA/OCA/AUP 1915 file, Joseph Chambers to Henry Parkinson 25 October 1915

[30] See Michael Snape, *God and the British Soldier: Religion and the British Army in the First and Second World Wars*, Routledge, London, 2005

[31] Finlay, p 168

[32] Vickers, p 331

[33] Downside Abbey Archives: Rawlinson Papers (Downside:Rawlinson) Correspondence with Bishops and Superiors, Stephen Rawlinson to Richard Collins, Bishop of Hexham & Newcastle 23 September 1918; Stephen Rawlinson to Edward Ilsley, Archbishop of Birmingham 14 October 1918

[34] Downside:Rawlinson Correspondence with Bishops and Superiors, Stephen Rawlinson to Mr G Monk, War Office, 29 April 1917

[35] Purdy, p 45

[36] Finlay, p 169

[37] Southwark Archdiocesan Archives, *The Southwark Record*, vol 15, No 4, 1936

[38] Finlay, p 190 – 1

[39] Obituary *The Oscotian Magazine*, 1923, pp 148 - 151

[40] Obituary *The Oscotian Magazine*, 1923 p 151

[41] Obituary, *Archdiocese of Birmingham Catholic Directory* 1924

[42] Catholic Bishopric of the Forces Archives (BFA) Eric Green File, 5 August 1914

[43] Snape, p 90

[44] Snape, p 103

[45] BFA, Charles Smith File

[46] BFA, Charles Smith File

[47] Downside:Rawlinson, Correspondence relating to casualties and honours, 2 June 1916

[48] Downside:Rawlinson, Correspondence to Bishops and Superiors, Joseph Whitfield to Stephen Rawlinson, 9 August 1916

[49] Downside:Rawlinson, Correspondence to Bishops and Superiors, Stephen Rawlinson to John Keily, Bishop of Plymouth, 25 November 1917

[50] Downside Rawlinson, Correspondence relating to casualties and honours, 15 March 1917

[51] BAA/OCA/ AUP 1921-1924 files

[52] BFA, Charles Smith File (parish history)

[53] Obituary *The Oscotian Magazine*, Summer 1955, pp 74 – 75

[54] BFA Charles McDonnell File

[55] BAA/OCA2/9/16/5/M/56 Charles McDonnell to Henry Parkinson, 19 February 1917

[56] Obituary, *Archdiocese of Birmingham Catholic Directory* 1928

[57] Finlay, p 171

[58] James Hagerty, *Benedictine Military Chaplains in the First World War*, English Benedictine Congregation History Commission Symposium, 1998, p 3

[59] Downside:Rawlinson, Correspondence A-L Samuel Gosling to Fr Young, March - April 1916

[60] Finlay, p 173

[61] BFA BF/2/1 Folder 3B Box 3, Cardinal Secretary of State to Cardinal Hinsley, 5 June 1935

[62] For accounts of the lives of Catholic chaplains, see Tom Johnstone and James Hagerty, *The Cross on the Sword: Catholic Chaplains in the Forces*, Geoffrey Chapman, London, 1996

63 Snape, p 234

64 *The Tablet* 11 May 1918, p 608

65 *The Walsall Advertiser*, 16 October 1915

66 Jonathan Walker ed. *War Letters to a Wife*, Spellmount, London, 2001, p 85

67 Walker, *War Letters*, p 106

68 BAA OCA2/9/16/5/M/56 Charles McDonnell to Henry Parkinson, 19 February 1917

69 Diana M Scarisbrick, *My Dear Ralph: Letters of a Family at War*, Minerva Press, London, 1994 pp 179 – 80. Whitfield did fulfil a promise, made countless times by chaplains, to write to Mrs Scarisbrick should anything happen to her husband, and was able to reassure her that his injuries were not life-threatening. The editor of the letters acknowledged the family tradition, and records that 'Fr Whitfield was a brave man, and remained a revered friend until his death in 1961'.

70 BAA OS2/7/M/5, Memoir of John Molloy

71 BAA OS 2/7/M/6

72 BAA OS2/7/M/5

73 BAA OS 2/7/M/6

74 Obituary, *The Oscotian Magazine*, Spring 1937, pp 194 - 195

75 Obituary, *Birmingham Archdiocesan Directory*, 1938

76 Obituary, *The Oscotian Magazine*, July 1917

77 Downside: Rawlinson, Correspondence relating to casualties, George Craven to Stephen Rawlinson, 14 April 1917

78 BFA, George Craven to Mgr Manuel Bidwell, 7 August 1914

79 Downside: Rawlinson, George Craven to Stephen Rawlinson, 27 August 1916

80 Downside: Rawlinson, Col. Hewetson to Stephen Rawlinson, 14 October 1916

81 Downside: Rawlinson, George Craven to Stephen Rawlinson, 22 December 1916

82 *The Oscotian Magazine*, December 1915, p 64

83 Vickers, p 342

84 BAA D3521 Cardinal Bourne to Archbishop Ilsley, 21 January 1916

85 BAA D3537 Mgr Arthur Jackman, on behalf of Cardinal Bourne to Archbishop Ilsley 10 February 1916

86 BAA D3539 Mgr Arthur Jackman to Archbishop Ilsley, 12 February 1916

87 In December 1916, the Lloyd George coalition replaced that of Herbert Asquith

88 BAA D3748 Mgr Bidwell to Archbishop Ilsley, 10 February 1917

89 BAA D3749 Archbishop Thomas Whiteside to Archbishop Ilsley, 10 February 1917

90 BAA D4006, Fr Edward Periera to Archbishop Ilsley, 18 December 1917

91 Finlay, p 178

92 BAA D3789 Acta of the Bishops' Meeting at Oscott College, 17 March 1917

93 BAA D5496 Cardinal Bourne to Archbishop Ilsley, 14 November 1917

94 Vickers, p 342

95 I am grateful to the Binnell family, Henry and Emily Bullivent's descendants, for information, and to Ancestry.co.uk

96 BAA FHD/A/5 F H Drinkwater Diary

[97] BAA FHD/A/20 James Crichton Memoir of Drinkwater

[98] Ibid

[99] BAA FHD/A/5 F H Drinkwater Diary

[100] BAA FHD/A/3 F H Drinkwater to his sister Agnes, 13 August 1916

[101] Downside:Rawlinson, Correspondence with Bishops and Superiors, Stephen Rawlinson to Edward Ilsley, Archbishop of Birmingham, 14 October 1918

[102] During the 1914-18 war 8,981 DSOs were awarded: www.firstworldwar.com

[103] All details come from his obituary in *The Oscotian Magazine*, January 1918, pp 42-45

[104] BAA D3789 Acta of Bishops' Meeting at Oscott 17 March 1917

[105] *The Birmingham Gazette*, 29 March 1917

[106] *The Oscotian Magazine,* Easter 1918, pp 98 - 101

[107] BAA OS2/7/A/4 Marie Arnold to Henry Parkinson, 3 November 1918

[108] BAA/OCA 2/9/16/5/S/70 John Stokes to Henry Parkinson, 22 April 1917

[109] BAA/OCA 2/9/16/5/S/28 George Ayles-Waters to Henry Parkinson, 5 May 1918

[110] Downside:Rawlinson Correspondence with Bishops and Superiors, Stephen Rawlinson to James Dey, 20 October 1918

[111] BAA/OCA 2/9/16/5/S/28 George Ayles-Waters to Henry Parkinson, 5 May 1918

[112] Finlay, p 194

[113] BFA Charles McDonnell File

[114] BAA/OCA 2/9/16/5/S/28 George Ayles-Waters to Henry Parkinson, 5 May 1918

[115] Ibid

[116] BAA AUP file 1918, Godric Kean to Henry Parkinson, 2 November 1918

[117] BAA/OCA 2/9/16/5/s/28 George Ayles-Waters to Henry Parkinson, 5 May 1918

[118] Information kindly supplied by Fr David Lannon, Salford Diocesan Archivist

[119] BAA/OCA 2//11/3/G/27 Samuel Gosling to Henry Parkinson, 1 February 1917

[120] BAA/OCA/ 2/11/3/G/27 Samuel Gosling to Henry Parkinson, 15 January 1917; BAA/OCA/2/9/16/5/M/56 Charles McDonnell to Henry Parkinson, 19 February 1917; BAA/OCA/2/9/16/5/A/28, George Ayles-Waters to Henry Parkinson, 5 May 1918

[121] Charles Plater, *The Priest and Social Action*, Longmans, London, 1914, p 108

[122] Plater, p 200

[123] Plater, p 174

[124] Kester Aspden, *Fortress Church the English Roman Catholic Bishops and Politics 1903-63*, Gracewing, Leominster, 2002 , p 45

[125] Obituary, *The Harvest,* March 1941

[126] BAA/OCA 2//11/3/G/27 Samuel Gosling to Henry Parkinson, 15 January 1917

[127] BAA/OCA 2/9/16/5/M/56 Charles McDonnell to Henry Parkinson, 3 April 1919

[128] Aspden, p 126

[129] Walker, *Letters*, pp 207 - 8

[130] Aspden, pp 122 – 4

[131] Quoted in Vickers, p 445

[132] BAA/OCA 2/1/3 Oscott College Diary 1901-32

[133] Finlay, p 312

[134] BAA/OCA 2/9/16/5/A/28 George Ayles-Waters to Henry Parkinson, 5 May 1918

[135] BAA/OCA 2/9/16/5/W/65 Osmund Woods to Henry Parkinson, 23 February 1916

[136] BAA/OCA 2/9/16/5/W/65 Osmund Woods to Henry Parkinson, 21 January 1919

[137] Obituary James Wharton, *The Oscotian Magazine*, 1966, pp 20-21

[138] BAA/OCA 2/1/3 Oscott College Diary 1901-32

[139] Williams, pp 58-9

[140] The Oscotian Magazine, Christmas 1927, p 80

[141] PDF ed. Phil Watson, *Birmingham Botany Collections: Mosses*, Birmingham Museums, 2013

[142] See *The Tablet*, Easter 2015

[143] Downside:Rawlinson Material collected for proposed book, P O'Hanlon to Stephen Rawlinson, 21 March 1928

[144] Williams, p 66

[145] Williams, p 66 – 7

[146] *The Walsall Advertiser*, 27 February 1915

[147] Garrett Sweeney, *St Edmund's House, Cambridge, the first eighty years: a history*, pub. privately, 1980, p 50

[148] Sweeney, p 51

[149] Quoted in Sweeney, p 51, no reference.

[150] John Sharp, 'Williams, Thomas Cuthbert Leighton (1877–1946)', *Oxford Dictionary of National Biography*, Oxford University Press, 2004

[http://www.oxforddnb.com/view/article/65568, accessed 18 July 2015]

[151] Obituary, *The Oscotian Magazine*, December 1946

[152] BFA BF2/1 Box 3, Dey File

[153] BFA BF2/1 Box 3, Dey File, Will, 11 May 1946

[154] BFA BF/2/1 Folder 3B Box 3 Dey File 15 July 1946

[155] BFA BF/2/1 Folder 3B box 3 Dey File, Fr Hugh Condon to Bishop Francis Walmesley, 3 August 1988

[156] Obituary, *The Oscotian Magazine*, December 1946

[157] BFA BF2/1 Box 3, Dey File, Notes by Samuel J Gosling

[158] Obituary, *The Oscotian Magazine*, Summer 1951, pp 50 - 51

[159] Obituary, *Birmingham Archdiocesan Directory,* 1951

[160] *The Oscotian Magazine*, Spring 1931 pp 37-38

[161] Obituary, *The Tablet*, 27 November 1954, p 20

[162] James Dey, 'The Church and the Land', in Hilaire Belloc, *Flee to the Fields*, Heath Cranton, London, 1934, p 144

[163] Race Matthews, 'Hilaire Belloc, Gilbert and Cecil Chesterton and the Making of Distributism', *Recusant History*, vol 30, 2010, p 313

[164] Finlay, p 2

[165] Walker, *Letters*, p 207-8

Index

aerial photography 63
Amery, Fr Walter 15, 96
Apostolic Union of Secular Clergy 15-16, 17, 27
Archer-Shee, Lt Col Sir Martin 102
Archer-Shee, Lt George 11-12, 102
Archer-Shee, Maj. 12
Archer-Shee, Martin 11-12, 102
Armistice Day 24, 78, 80
Arnold, Lt Joseph 71, 95
Arnold, Marie 71
Arras, Battle of 43
Arras Memorial 41
Artillery Wood Cemetery 103
Arts and Crafts Movement 90
Auchy 63
Avesnes le Compte Cemetery, 103
Ayles-Waters, Fr George 74, *75*, 76, 80, 96

Bagneux British Cemetery 103
Bagshawe, Capt. Edward 102
Bagshawe, Judge William 102
Barber, Stephen 99
Barry, Fr William 14, 65, 89
Basra War Cemetery 21, 55
Beaconsfield 27
Beaumont College 25
Belgian army 17
Belgian refugees 13-14, 17, 25
Belgium, German invasion 12
Belloc, Hilaire 90, 93
Benedict XV 12, 32
Bennett, Lt Col George 9
Berkeley, Captain Hubert 99
Berkeley, Lt Col. T. Mowbray 99

Bernaerts, Lt Joseph *16,* 17, 95
Bethune 63
Bethune Casualty Clearing Station 45
Bidwell, Mgr Manuel 25, 28, 58
Birmingham Museum 82
Birmingham, University of 7
Black and Tans 10
Black Watch 34, 43, 47
Bligh, James 21, 99
Blundell, Eustace 99
Boniface, Fr George 96
Bourne, Cardinal Francis: Catholic Social Teaching 79; chaplain applications 25, 28; chaplain numbers 24; Collins, Fr Herbert 42-3; conscription 58-9; 16th Irish Division chaplains *49*; stance on war 6; War Office negotiations 58
British Army of the Rhine 87, 98
British Expeditionary Force 21, 29, 34, 84
British Newspaper Archive 5
Britten, Lt Col Thomas 20-1, 94
Brown's Road Military Cemetery *64*
Browne, Fr John O'Riordan 17-8, 96
Buckfast Abbey 27
Buckfastleigh 27
Bullivent, Henry and Emily 60-1, *91*
Bunce, Fr William *40*, 41, 96
burial controversies 26
Butler, Cecily 32
Byrne, Fr M. *86*

Cabaret-Rouge British Cemetery 45, 54
Cambrai Cathedral *73*
Cambrin Military Cemetery 103
Cameron Highlanders 47

Carlisle, Fr George *9*, 96

Carson, Sir Edward 12

Casartelli, Bishop 17, 78

Castle Bromwich airfield 57

Caswell, Canon John 14

Catholic Land Association 90-2

Catholic Land Movement 92, 93

Catholic School for Social Science 78

Catholic Social Guild 15, 77, 79, 91

Catholic Social Teaching 15, 77-8, 90, 92, 93

Catholic Women's League 6, 31, 32

Chambers, Fr Joseph 20

Chesterton, G.K. 27, 83, 90, 93

civilian casualties 76

Coldstream Guards 32, 103

Colegrave, Lt Gerald 102

Coleman, Jerome 21, 99

Collins, Fr Herbert: character 42-5; death 43; family background 42; grave 45, *54*; obituary 43-5; Oscott record 42, *44*, 94, 96; subdeacon *9*

Collins, Fr J. *86*

Cologne 87

Commonwealth (Imperial) War Graves Commission 5, 64, 70

Communism 77, 92

Connaught Rangers 32, 84, 103

conscription: Acts 58; chaplain substitute 59; clergy exemptions 31, 58-9; Ireland 58; seminarians 58-60; War Office 58-9

Cotton College 24, 28, 40, 47, 84, 86

Craven, Fr George: after war *86;* appointed bishop 46, 55; casualty stations 45-6; Crusade of Rescue 46; decorations *55;* Herbert Collins obituary 43-5; volunteers as chaplain 45, 97

Crawford, Col Raymond 99

Crichton, Mgr James 65, 83

Crimean War 10

Cronin, Fr Charles 83

Croston Hall 104

Crusade of Rescue 42, 46

Davis, Mgr Francis 87, 88

Dease, Capt. Maurice 102

Dease, Edmund and Katherine 102

de Capitain, Canon Francis de 88, 89

de la Fontaine, Lt Col Victor 67-8, 94

demobilisation 78-9

de Mussy, Francois 103

de Mussy, Henri 103

de Mussy, Philippe 103

de Trafford, Cuthbert 104

de Trafford, Galfrid 104

de Trafford, Lt Ralph 104

de Trafford, Lt Reginald 104

Dey, Fr James: Apostolic Union 16; bequests 88; Bishop of the Forces 87, *88*; British Expeditionary Force 84; Cambridge 86; Catholic Land Association 91-2; Catholic Social Teaching 90; Cotton College 87-8; East Africa Force 85; Eucharistic fast 73-4; family background 84; military hospitals 86; obituary 87, 89; Oscott Rector 84, 86, 87, 88-9; portrait *50*; regular army 84, 97; St Edmund's Ware, 86; Vicar General 85

d'Hollander, Honore Adolphe 17, 101

Distributism 90, 93

Donleavy, Rev. William 97

Dormer, Captain the Hon Charles 99

Dormer, Lt Gen. Sir James 9

Dorran, Rev. William 97

Douglas-Dick, Brig.-Gen. Archibald 99

Downside Abbey 5

Drinkwater, Agnes 65

Drinkwater Fl. Lt Oscar: character 62-3; joins RFC 62; Oscott, 62-3; marriage 63; memorial 95; schooling 62; shot down 63; graves 64

Drinkwater, Fr Francis: brother's bones 64; diary 62, 63, 65; letters 65-6; gassed and wounded *53*, 62; military record 97; Molloy, John 41; Nondescript Club *11*; photo *51, 86*; *Sower, The* 65, 89; Theologians football team *10*

Drinkwater, Fr John *40, 86*

Dugmore, Lt Col William 61, 94
Dunn, Fr Joseph 88
Durham Light Infantry 102
Dwyer, Fr Joseph *11*, 23-4, *40*, 97

East Africa Force 85
Easter Rising 12
East Lancs Regiment 104
East Surrey Regiment 67
Emery, Fr Augustine 16
English College, Rome 16, 59, 83
Ervilles *49*
Esmonde, Captain John 99
Esmonde, Midshipman John 102
Eucharistic fast 73-4

Farrell, Captain John 99
Farrell, Col. Edward 99
Farren, Lt William 18, 19, 95
Father Hudson's Homes 41, 46
Feilding, Col Rudolph 99
Feilding, Hon. Everard 99
Feilding, Lt Col Rowland 32-3, 78, 93
Feilding, Rudolph and Everard 32
Fielding, Lt Commander Hugh, 102
Finlay, Katherine 6, 19
Fitzgerald, Brig.-Gen. Percy 99
Fitzgerald, Captain Gerald 102
Fitzgerald, Hon. J.D. 102
Fitzherbert-Brockholes, Captain Thomas 102
Fitzherbert-Brockoles, William 102
Fitzherbert, Captain the Hon. Thomas 99
Fitzherbert, Rear Admiral Edward 99
Flee to the Fields, 92, 93
Fletcher, Robert 102
Fletcher, 2nd Lt Arthur 102
Flinn, Fr William 22
Foley, Rev. Wilfred 97
Foster, Fr Stewart 34

Fraser, Major the Hon. Hugh 99
Fuller, Maj. 25
Furniss, Fr Frederick 19

Gallipoli 22, 24, 104
Gardner, Lt Leslie 21, 99
Garrison Artillery 40
general absolution 23
George V, King 39
Geraghty, Joseph 17
German prisoners of war 26, *33*, 85
Ghent 16, 17
Gilshennan, Lt Christopher 21, 99
Gloucestershire Regiment 20, 104
Goris, Paul-Maria 17, 101
Gosling, Fr Samuel *9*, 16, 30, 89-90, 97
Grattan-Bellew, Brig.-Gen. Sir H. 99
Grattan-Bellew, Henry 103
Grattan-Bellew, Maj. William 103
Grattan-Esmonde, Brig-Gen. Laurence 100
Grattan-Esmonde 2nd Lt Geoffrey 100
Grattan Esmonde, Sir Thomas 102
Great Game of Bandy 10
Great Western Railway 40
Green, Fr Eric 24, 97
Griffin, Fr Bernard 46

Hagerty, James 5
Haig, Field Marshal Sir Douglas 39
Harrington, Peter 5
Heenan, Cardinal John 46
Heffernan, Leading Seaman 100
Helles Memorial 104
Herbert, Maj.-Gen. Sir Ivor 100
Hewetson, Col 46
Hickie, James 10
Hickie, Maj. Gen. W. 10, 100
Hinsley, Cardinal Arthur 30, *88*
Houplines Communal Cemetery 102

Howley, John and William 19
Howley, Lt Col Henry 100
Howley, Maj. Jasper 19-20, 94
Howley, William, Gerard, Richard, Henry 19
Hyde Park Corner Cemetery, Belgium 48, 95
Hymers, Fr Edward 87

Ilsley, Archbishop Edward 6-7, 28, 58, 59, 87
Imperial War Museum 5
Indian Army 20
Invincible, HMS 102
Ireland 58
Isaacs, Sir Rufus 12
Italian Expeditionary Force 78

Jackman, Mgr 58
Jackson, Henry *60*, 61
Jackson, Joe 61
Jarvis, Fr Ernest 97

Kean, Fr Godric 16
Keatinge, Bishop William: Armistice 80; Assistant Principal Chaplain 29; chaplains' placement 23; military bishop 30; portrait 30; Rawlinson, Dom Stephen 29
Kelly, Catherine and James 69
Kelly, Private Leo 69-70, 95
Kenilworth 14
Kew Gardens 82
Kiely, Bishop 25
King's Own Rifles 63
Knox, Mgr Ronald 83
Krauth, Clement *9*

La Laiterie Cemetery 102
Landovery Castle, HMHS 23-4
Law, Maj. Gen. Victor 9
Le Touret Military Cemetery 104
Leamington Spa 14
Leese, Col W. 100

Leo XIII 15, 77, 93
Leuven/Louvain, 13-14
Lewis, James 21, 100
Lincolnshire Regiment 20
Lockett, Fr Francis 28, *40*, 98
Lomax, Fr Joseph *9*, 78, 98
Longueville, Lt Col Reginald 100
Loos, Battle of 43, 67
Lynch, Captain Thomas 100

Magrath, Gerald 100
Mahratta Light Infantry 20
Mailly Wood Cemetery 104
Manchester Cemetery, Pas de Calais 71
Manchester Regiment 71
Mann, William 21, 100
Maxwell-Stuart, Edmund 11, 103
Maxwell-Stuart, Edmund jnr, Henry, Joseph, Alfred 11, 103
Maxwell-Stuart, Lt Joseph 103
May Laws 19
McClymont, Richard 100
McCrae, John 93
McDonnell, Fr Charles: Arnold, Lt Joseph 71; at Oscott *10, 11*; Catholic Social Teaching 78; communion hosts and wine 74; funerals 38; Italy posting 78; obituary 29; Royal Dublin Fusiliers 28; soldiers' faith 33, 37-8; volunteers 28, 98
McIntyre, Archbishop John 82
McKenna, James 21, 100
McMahon, Fr Francis 98
McNabb OP, Fr Vincent 93
McNeill, Fr John 47-8
McSwiney, James 100
McVickers, 2nd Lt Alfred 100
Mechlen/Malines Cathedral 14
Menin Gate 12, 104
Mentana, Battle of 104
military chaplains: applications 25; appointments 23-4; burials *26*; deaths 22,

24, 76; devastated churches 28, 36, *66, 73,* 74; general absolution 23; German POWs *33, 85;* guidelines for 29; hospital staff 46; inter-faith tensions 26; key role 23; morale 73-6; navy 23; officers' support 32; placement 22-3, 35; numbers 21-2, 24; religious orders 23; service hardships 28, 37, 73-6, 84; training 31; volunteers 22-3

Molloy, John: Bunce. William 41; character 40-1; death 41; faith 40-1; leaves Oscott 40; memorial 95; Nondescript Club *11;* Philosophers' football team *40;*

Mons retreat, 84

Moore, Ruby 63

Moriarty, Bishop James *88*

Morris, William 90, 92

Mostyn, Captain Piers 103

Mostyn, Fr Edward 23, 98

Mostyn, Lt Col Edward 100

Mulligan, Fergus 5

Murphy, Captain Edward 103

Murphy, Jerome 103

Museum of Army Chaplaincy 5

Museum of Natural History 82

Neuve Chapelle 20

Newman, John Henry 77

Nicholson, Maj. Edward 103

Noel, Col Hon. Edward 69, 100

Nondescript Club 11

North Staffordshire Regiment 61

North Wales Territorials 17

Nugent, Captain the Hon William 103

O'Connell, Fr Timothy 98

Oratory School, Birmingham 59

Osborne Naval College 12

Oscotian Day 69

Oscotian Society 20

Oscotian, The: casualty lists 47; College activities 8; Collins, Fr Herbert 42; heating College 57; volunteers 21; war deaths 9, 19;

Whitfield article 34-9

Oscott College: blackout curtains 57; cemetery 61; chapel 5, *8, 56;* electric light 27; farm work 61, 69; Feast 11; impact of war 8-12; military tradition 8-12; orchestra 27; Philosophers' football team *40;* post-war reforms 80-2, 83; requisition risk 7; school closure 8; seminary formation; student volunteers 17-9; Theologians' football team *10;* 'unsatisfactory spirit' 81; war deaths 19-21, 57, 68, 69-70; war memorial 17, 18, 20, 21, 45, 48, 61, 64, 68, 70, 71, 72; war privations 57, 68-9

Oscott Publications 5

Oudenaard Cemetery 16

Ovillers 26

Oxford Dictionary of National Biography 5

pacifism 15

Parkinson, Mgr Henry: Apostolic Union 15-16,17; army recruitment 15, 18; Arnold, Lt Joseph 71; Catholic Social Teaching 15; conscription 59; correspondence 5, 15-16, 17, 18, 27; death 83; death of Bart Scanlon 47-8; formation 15; Oscott final years 82; portrait *52;* post-war social ills 91; Stokes, John 72; Vice-Rector and Rector 15; war speech 31

Paul, St 24

Pell, Elizabeth 102

Pereira, Fr Edward 59

Petre, Laurence 100

Philips VC, Everard Lisle 9

Pike, Lt Col Cuthbert 100

Pius XI 90

Pius XII 30, 92

Plater SJ, Fr Charles 15, 77, 79

Poperinghe Military Cemetery 103

Portsmouth Naval Memorial 102

Poziers Memorial 70

Prendergast, Lt Col Gerard 100

Priest and Social Action, The 77

Primer of Social Science, A 77

Prospect Hill Cemetery, Gouy 72

Quadraegesimo Anno 90
Queen's Own Oxfordshire Hussars 104

Radcliffe, Captain Arthur 103
Radcliffe, Henry 100
Radcliffe, Lt Col Philip 100
Railway Dugouts Burial Ground 61
Ratio of prayers 16, 27
Rattigan, Terence 12
Rawlinson, Dom Stephen 29-30, 45, 66, 73, 80
Reformation 13
Reninghelst New Military Cemetery 68, 94, 103
Rerum Novarum 15, 77, 90
Rhodes, Fr Philip *56,* 59, 82
Robbins, Harold 91-2
Rogers, Steve 5
Ross, Sub-Lt Leonard 21, 100
Rowan, Fr John 14
Royal Air Force 85
Royal Army Medical Corps 21, 58
Royal Dublin Fusiliers 28, 72
Royal Engineers 103, 104
Royal Fleet Auxiliary 21
Royal Fleet Reserve 24
Royal Flying Corps 63, 103
Royal Fusiliers 10, 102, 104
Royal Garrison Artillery 21
Royal Irish Rifles Graveyard 104
Royal Marine Artillery 21
Royal Marine Light Infantry 104
Royal Naval Division 21, 24
Royal Naval Volunteer Reserve 21, 24
Royal Welsh Fusiliers 18
Rue Petillon Military Cemetery 20
Ruskin, John 90
Russell, Michael 21, 100
Ryan, Captain James 103
Ryan, Fr Arthur 69
Ryan, John J. 100

Ryan, Maj. Clement 103
Ryan, Walter 103

Sailly-Labourse *48*
Salonika 24
Sandhurst 20
Scanlon, Sergeant Bartholomew: family background 47; grave *47, 48*; joins army 47; memorial 95; Oscott record 47; promotion 48;
Scarisbrick, Captain Stuart 39
Seafield War Hospital 18
Sempels, Joseph-Marie 17
Sempels, Victor 17
Senior Chaplain's Office 22
Shaiba 20
Sharp, Fr John 5
Shepard, Maj. Thomas 101
Shepherd, 2nd Lt Bernard 104
Sibeth, Charles Joseph 104
Sibeth, 2nd Lt Charles 104
Silvertop, Henry 104
Silvertop, 2nd Lt Francis 104
Slaughter, Lt Col Reginald 101
Slim, Prob. Surgeon Charles 101
Smith, Mgr Charles: Apostolic Union 16; decorations 51; inter-faith tensions 26-7; volunteers as chaplain 25, 98
Smyth, Maj. Robert 101
Snape, Michael 5
Somme, Battle of 39
South African War 20, 67
South Midland Ambulance Service 30
South Staffordshire Regiment 11, 104
Sower, The 65, 89
S. Sulpice, Paris 45
Stafford, Fr 68
Stanton, 2nd Lt Robert 101
Stapleton-Bretherton, Edith 32
St Bede's College Manchester, 18

St Chad's Cathedral 14, 45
St Charles' House, Oxford 87
St Edmund's House, Cambridge 34, 39, 86
St Edmund's College, Ware 34, 42, 84, 86
St Joseph's School, Leeds 71
St Mary on the Quay Bristol 12
St Mary the Mount, Walsall 31
St Mary's Levenshulme 78
St Mary's College Holywell 17
Stokes, Lance-Corporal John 72, 95
St Omer 18
Stonor, 2nd Lt Cuthbert 104
Stonor, Hon. Howard 104
Stonor, Lt Edward 101
Stonyhurst College 18
St Patrick's Wolverhampton 29
St Peblig Churchyard 18
St Synphorien Military Cemetery 102
Sumner, 2nd Lt Ernest 101
Sumner, Francis 9
Sumner, Lt George 101

Tablet, The 31, 65
Talbot, Lt Reginald 101
Templeux le Guerard Cemetery 104
Traill, Fr Randolph 22, 98
Treowen, Maj. Gen. Lord 101
Turner, George 32

Ushaw College 18

van den Broek, Canon Henri 14
van der Velde, Robert 17
van Trimpont, Ferdinand 101
Victoria, Queen 20
Victory, HMS, 104
Villers-au-Flos 71
von Trimpont, Ferdinand 17

Wadsworth, Nurse Edith 76
War Graves Photographic Project 5
War Letters to a Wife 32
War of Independence, Ireland 10
War Office 25, 28, 29, 58
Weedall Chantry 9, 12
Weeford Cottage 92
Wells, Frank 68
Welman, Henry Acton 104
Welman, Lt Henry 104
Westminster Cathedral 6
Weston, 2nd Lt James 101
Whiteside, Archbishop 59
Whitfield, Fr Joseph: Anglican chaplains 26;
Cambridge 87; character and background 34;
decorations 39; final years 39; Vice-Rector
34, 83; war experiences 35; wounded 39
Williams, Archbishop Thomas 56, 86, 87, 88,
89, 91, 98
Williams, Mgr Michael 83
Williamson, Fr Benedict 79
Wilson, Cyril 101
Wilson, President Woodrow 14
Wimereux General Hospital 46
Winslow Boy, The 12
Withers, Fr Brian 86
Withers, Fr W. 86
Wolseley, Edward Talbot 104
Wolseley, 2nd Lt William 104
Woodchester, Glos 12
Woods, Fr Osmund 42, 81, 98
Woodward, Col Charles 104
Woodward, Lt Charles 104
World's Debate, The 14

Ypres, 84

Zouaves 104